D0313079

NEWNESS OF LIFE

— an illustrated Confirmation Course

by

BRIAN MOUNTFORD

Vicar of Christ Church, Southgate

FOREWORD
by Bishop Bill Westwood

MOWBRAY
LONDON & OXFORD

Copyright © Brian Mountford 1984

ISBN 0 264 67013 2

First published 1984
by A. R. Mowbray & Co. Ltd,
Saint Thomas House, Becket Street,
Oxford, OX1 1SJ

Typeset by Oxford Publishing Services, Oxford
Printed in Great Britain

British Library Cataloguing in Publication Data

Mountford, Brian
  Newness of life.
  1. Confirmation—Study and teaching
  I. Title
  248.4   BV815
ISBN 0–264–67013–2

FOREWORD

by the Rt Revd Bill Westwood, Bishop of Edmonton
(Bishop designate of Peterborough)

One of the strange things about being a Bishop is that you very rarely face the same way as the congregation. This is especially true in a Confirmation. A full church of candidates, family and friends sit, stand and kneel facing the East end and the Bishop finds his 'centre of holy attention' not in the great traditional places of altar and cross but in the faces of those he is to confirm.

More and more of these candidates are older and their commitment and courage cannot be doubted. At the age of 30, 40, even 60 and 70, to stand before the congregation and then kneel before the Bishop requires a confident living faith. The younger, coming perhaps from a class in school or a street on an Estate where they are the only committed Christians, have to have something deep inside them which impels them to this step and keeps them strong in it. I am conscious of confirming a very committed band of Christians in these days.

However, the promises laid upon them by the new Service call not only for a commitment of the heart but also for the assent of the mind. I believe that Brian Mountford's book, springing as it does out of his own faith and his experience as a parish priest, will help to equip Confirmation candidates in these days with a well-established personal faith and a reason for that which is in them.

I believe that those who use it will be better enabled to make their promises as they come to their Confirmation and will go on into the rich life of the Church better formed in faith and ready to learn both spiritually and intellectually.

September 1984   +BILL EDMONTON

CONTENTS

PREFACE

When someone says that they have become a Christian, or been confirmed, it is often with a sense of having arrived, almost as if there were no more to be done. But this moment of decision is only the beginning of a spiritual journey and, like all journeys, as you travel the scenery changes. No one should expect their Christian experience to stand still in a fixed and unchangeable form, because if it does it will stagnate. Instead one needs to be open to the guidance of the Holy Spirit and ready to learn from the experience of others. That is why even those religious discussions that seem to get nowhere are in fact very useful, because they give us the chance to put our spiritual ideas into words, and to listen to others trying to do the same.

Another major resource for Christian development is reading, and there are a large number of books in which writers describe their own experiences in making the Christian journey.

Newness of Life is intended either as a handbook for confirmation preparation itself, or as a first book after confirmation. It consolidates what has been studied in confirmation preparation by discussing some of the basic questions that Christians need to think about. It is also a stepping off point for further reading, and hopefully it will provide the stimulation to explore different aspects of Christian belief more deeply.

Throughout the book there are 'boxed' ideas for discussion and activity. These are intended primarily for use in groups, on the supposition that the majority of parishes will have groups for those wanting to learn more about the Christian life. Belonging to a group like this is helpful whether the participants are teenagers or adults, and generally the ideas should be appropriate to either age range.

I am grateful to Mrs Lesley Barlow, Headmistress of Woolmore Primary School, Poplar, for her extensive help in providing material for these sections.

I must also thank Stephen Scrase of Photo Coverage, London, NW2 for taking many of the photographs specially for this book.

I also gratefully acknowledge permission to reproduce the following photographs: pp. 14 & 89 Popperfoto; p. 15 National Gallery; pp. 17, 29 & 35 Sonia Halliday Photographs; p. 22 Sister Daniel; p. 32 Zoological Society of London; p. 44 Graham Tatlock; p. 45 Wilkins Studios Ltd, Enfield; p. 65 Taizé Community; p. 72 Council for the Care of Churches; p. 76 USPG; p. 95 Imperial War Museum; p. 105 Press Association.

Extract from the Marriage Service in The Alternative Service Book 1980 is reproduced with permission of the Central Board of Finance of the Church of England.

The poem 'This bread I break was once the oat' from *The Poems* by Dylan Thomas (J.M. Dent & Sons Ltd) is reproduced by permission of David Higham Associates Ltd.

The verse from 'A Carol for the Universe' by Sydney Carter is © Stainer & Bell, and is reprinted with permission.

All biblical quotations are from the Revised Standard Version of the Bible, copyrighted 1946, 1953, © 1971, 1973 by the Division of Christian Education of the National Council of Churches of Christ in the USA.

B.M.

I. BELIEF IN GOD

'DEAR GOD, how come you're never on TV?' asks Kim in *Children's Letters to God* (Fontana). She has hit the nail on the head for many who find it difficult to believe in God. How do we know that he exists if we cannot see him? And how do we know that he loves us when we cannot experience from him the usual physical signs of affection like conversation, looks and touch?

There are obvious differences between our knowledge of God and our knowledge of what we call scientific 'facts'. For example, no one has difficulty in believing that the tides are caused by the gravitational pull of the moon because there is a physical explanation that is easy to accept as true, based on our common experience of gravity. However, this does not mean that belief in what can be rationally explained is superior to belief in something which remains a puzzle and cannot be seen — simply that they are different.

However difficult God may sometimes seem, it makes sense to take seriously the fact that millions of people have had experiences which they interpret as God working in their lives. Some typical instances of this kind of experience are: the feeling of personal humility when confronted by the vastness and beauty of nature; a prayer has been answered; the instinctive cry to God when faced with tragedy or pain; the build up of hints and intuitions that God is there, as the creative and loving force behind the universe.

It is usual for people who have such feelings about God to be convinced that what they have experienced is entirely real and genuine, and not to be

unduly disturbed by cynics who say 'Oh, you don't
believe all that nonsense, do you?' For basically,

**Religious experience is a very important part
of the human psychological make-up.**

---

religious experience is a very important part of the
human psychological make-up, and cannot be
ignored by science.

Equally, Christians cannot ignore science. It would
be silly, for example, to insist that a biblical
writer's version of an Old Testament event was
right, if archaeology showed it to be wrong. Both
science and Chrstianity are concerned with finding
the truth.

A matter of faith
Often in discussion about religious belief the
argument is pushed to the point where someone
will ask, 'But how do you know that that is true?'
Usually the reply is: 'Well, it is a matter of faith. I
simply believe that it is true'.

Then the discussion comes to a sort of crossroads
because what is really being said is that there are
some mysterious aspects of God which it is
impossible to express in limited human language.

The word 'faith' describes an attitude to God
which is daring, and does not rely on proof. It
refers to the personal trust that a Christian puts in
God as a result of learning about the life and
teaching of Jesus, and the acceptance that he is
Lord. When understood in this way faith is rather
like the feeling of confidence one person might
have in another. For example, when someone says
that they have faith in their doctor, it means that he
or she is confident that the doctor can make them

well. This feeling of confidence is based partly on the knowledge that the doctor is properly qualified, but probably more on the fact that he or she is someone who inspires trust as a person.

Sometimes 'faith' is used in another way, to describe the whole body of basic Christian teachings and doctrines. So that if one speaks for instance of the 'Catholic Faith' reference is being made to the traditional teachings of the Catholic part of the Church.

Is it wrong to have doubts?

Some Christians put an extremely heavy emphasis on the importance of having a strong faith in God. Occasionally this can be very worrying to the person who particularly wants to believe, but who finds that faith does not come easily or naturally. Such a person can easily feel guilty or inadequate in an atmosphere where the great majority seem to have a rock-solid faith. But is it right that anyone should feel guilty and inadequate in this way? The evidence is that relationships with God develop at a different pace and that for some people faith is the work of a lifetime, for others it comes in a flash.

Coming to terms with doubt often leads to greater faith.

Naturally, when thinking about the infinite power of God our limited human minds are bound to experience doubt, because we cannot understand his power and glory. So it is not wrong to have doubts. In fact, coming to terms with doubt in an honest way often leads to greater faith because it means that a person is approaching God realistically and openly.

Creeds

From time to time Christians have found it helpful to summarize their beliefs in a formal statement, called a creed. The word comes from the Latin and means 'belief'. In The Alternative Service Book 1980, in the Eucharist we say the Nicene Creed (ASB p. 123) and at Morning and Evening Prayer we say the Apostles' Creed (ASB pp. 57 and 58). These statements tell us what God is like and how he reveals himself.

The basis of all these creeds is expressed more straightforwardly in the Baptismal Creed, which is

---

Ideas for drama on the theme of 'God'.

The following ideas, and those at the end of this chapter, are suitable for use in a group of between four and fifteen people.

(a) Discuss what the shepherds' reaction might have been to the announcement by the angel that Jesus had been born in Bethlehem. (Luke 2.8–20). Why did they go to Bethlehem? What did they expect to see? What did they take with them? Try to reconstruct their conversation. Alternatively, act the Wakefield Shepherds Play by David Self (published by Macmillan Drama Script, price £1.50 from Samuel French, 52 Fitzroy Street, London, W1T 6JR). Either could be used as a nativity play in church, or suggest to the warden of your local old people's home or children's hospital that you perform the play there at Christmas time.

(b) God has had an amazing and transforming effect on the lives of many people. Think of someone for whom the effect has been dramatic, find out all you can about them and make a play based on their life. Some possibilities are:
Martin Luther King, Dietrich Bonhoeffer, Eric Liddell (made famous in *Chariots of Fire*), St Peter.

---

also used at confirmation (ASB p. 232). It asks three questions:

> 1. Do you believe and trust in God the Father, who made the world?

> 2. Do you believe and trust in his Son Jesus Christ, who redeemed mankind?

> 3. Do you believe and trust in his Holy Spirit, who gives life to the people of God?

The Father, Son, and Holy Spirit together make what is called the Holy Trinity. They are the three aspects or 'faces' of God which he has revealed to mankind in the course of history.

THE THREE FACES OF GOD

1. The Father who made the world

Jesus taught his disciples to think of God as their heavenly father when he showed them how to pray. He was referring, of course, to the God who had been worshipped by the Jewish people throughout their history.

They believed that God had created the world, and this is described in the first three chapters of Genesis. The creation story in Genesis is sometimes called the creation 'myth', because it seems to be a poetic or literary way of representing God's great creative power. Today the majority of people accept the scientific explanation of how the world and man came into being called 'the theory of evolution'. This maintains that life has developed over millions of years rather than the six days described in Genesis. This does not mean to say

The Earth as seen from a moon voyage

that Genesis was wrong, but that it is a primitive and poetic recognition by the people who wrote it that God is the force of creation behind the universe.

It is interesting to note that both St Paul and the writer of St John's gospel believed that Jesus Christ (whom St John refers to as the 'Word' — John 1. 1–5) existed from the beginning of time, and that God's creative power worked through him. Although they are difficult passages, it is worth looking at John 1. 1–5 and Colossians 1. 15–20.

2. The Son who redeems mankind

From very early times Jesus' followers came to believe that he was the Son of God. St Mark begins his gospel with a statement to this effect: 'The beginning of the gospel of Jesus Christ, the Son of God'.

The belief that Jesus Christ was the Son of God led on to the idea that he was actually God in the form of a human being. As St John puts it: 'The Word became flesh and dwelt among us' (John 1. 13). This remarkable belief is called the doctrine of the 'incarnation', which means quite simply, the embodiment of God in human flesh. The incarnation is celebrated particularly at Christmas, and many of the Christmas carols speak about it. Look, for instance, at 'Hark! the herald-angels sing', 'In the bleak mid-winter', and Sydney Carter's 'A Carol for the Universe'.

HARK! THE HERALD-ANGELS SING

> '. . . Veiled in flesh the Godhead see!
> Hail, the incarnate deity!
> Pleased as Man with man to dwell,
> Jesus, our Emmanuel.'

IN THE BLEAK MID-WINTER

> '. . . Our God, heaven cannot hold him,
> Nor earth sustain;
> Heaven and earth shall flee away
> When he comes to reign:
> In the bleak mid-winter
> A stable place sufficed
> The Lord God Almighty,
> Jesus Christ.'

A CAROL FOR THE UNIVERSE

> '. . . When the King of all creation
> had a cradle on the earth,
> Holy was the human body,
> Holy was the human birth:'

The Adoration of the Shepherds, painting by Renni

15

Obviously if Jesus Christ is God incarnate our knowledge of his life and work gives us a direct insight into what God is like. Indeed, in St John's gospel (14.9) Jesus says: 'He who has seen me has seen the Father'. By looking at Jesus we can see that God is forgiving, loving, able to heal the sick, willing to make great sacrifices for us, humble, has power over evil and has power over nature.

But why was it necessary for God to become man in the first place? The answer is that man's sinfulness had created such a barrier between God and man that their relationship had broken down. Jesus came to change this, and the baptismal creed describes the process of setting man in a right relationship with God as the Son 'redeeming' mankind.

Redemption creates a picture of slaves and their desire for freedom, because to 'redeem' a slave meant to pay his master enough money to buy him out of bondage. In this case we are asked to imagine human beings as slaves to sin, unable to free themselves, almost like drug addicts who, much as they would like to, cannot break the habit. Furthermore, the inevitable results of this slavery to sin is death. What Jesus does is to buy us out of slavery by paying with his own life at the crucifixion, and so we receive freedom and eternal life.

These ideas will be found in many hymns. Look, for instance, at the popular hymn 'Living Lord'. It describes Jesus as:

'Led out to die on Calvary,
risen from death to set us free'

and the hymn 'A Man there lived in Galilee' talking of the crucifixion says:

'No thought can gauge the weight of woe
on him, the sinless, laid;
We only know that with his blood
our ransom price was paid'

The Crucifixion, painting by Giotto, Lower Church Assisi, Italy, (14th century)

Atonement simply means the at-one-ment of God and man.

You will have to decide whether this picture of redemption explains satisfactorily what we call the 'atonement'. Atonement sounds difficult but simply means the at-one-ment of God and man. Do not despair there are other attempts to picture and explain the nature of Jesus Christ's saving work, because not surprisingly Christians have been trying to puzzle it out since the time when the New Testament was being written.

(a) *Christ is punished for sin instead of us*

This is an idea that was developed by St Anselm, Archbishop of Canterbury in the eleventh century. It is that humans, because of their sin, deserve to be punished by death, and that God, being just, cannot do anything but demand that that penalty is paid. However, because he is not only just but also loving, he sends his own son to bear the punishment of death on behalf of all mankind.

This popular theory is often compared with a landowner who is owed rent by his tenants, but they are too poor to pay. If they do not pay, of course, they will be thrown into prison. But the generous and just landowner solves the problem by sending each of them exactly the right amount of money to pay their debts, and justice is satisfied.

It is a theory which is not unlike redemption from slavery, in the sense that in both cases God requires a price to be paid for sin. Yet surely God could be merciful of his own free will without insisting on the gruesome suffering of his Son, and does it not make a nonsense of the doctrine of the Holy Trinity, which says that Father, Son and Holy Spirit are exactly equal partners in the Godhead, if the Father is an autocratic landlord and the Son a payment in his pocket? Questions such as these have led some Christians to look for a different explanation of atonement.

(b) *Christ's suffering is a proof of God's love*

This is not a new idea either. Peter Abelard, who wrote at the beginning of the twelfth century, was its first great exponent. Basically it says that Christ's death is a demonstration of God's willingness to go to the limits of suffering for his people.

No sacrifice is too great for our loving God, and the fact that Christ rose from the dead is a proof of God's power over death. Such a picture of God's suffering in Christ might well move us to repent of

---

No sacrifice is too great for our loving God.

---

our sins and put our trust in him, just as it did the so-called 'good' thief on the cross, and presumably the soldier who said when Christ died, 'Truly this man was a son of God'.

If one wanted a modern parable for this idea, you might think of a surgeon who is faced with an extremely difficult operation. After seven hours in the operating theatre he has expended every ounce of physical and mental energy to save a patient's life, so that when it is over he has to be helped from the theatre by his assistants.

Critics will say that this is all very well, but it does not explain how the death and resurrection of Christ actually *effects* our salvation or makes it happen. It is an example of God's love, not a once and for all decisive act. Yet does God need a decisive act, or does he simply need to convince us that we must put our faith in him to find eternal life?

(c) *God shares our experience, we share his*

This idea is related to the previous one, but has perhaps a greater sense of cause and effect about it. It is simply that because God in Christ shared our human experience, even the misery of a slow and painful death, we are able to share in his life of eternal fulfilment. It is as though the incarnation itself bridges the gap between human and divine experience.

(d) Christ fights the devil and wins

The devil stands for all that is evil, and in his death and resurrection Christ took on evil and conquered it once and for all, so that Christians may now live a new life unencumbered by the burdens of sin. This so-called 'classic' theory provides a picture of a cosmic battle between good and evil. Interestingly it is also present in the early ministry of Jesus, particularly as portrayed by Mark. At the beginning of his ministry Jesus was driven into the wilderness to be 'tempted by Satan'. The wilderness was the natural home of evil spirits according to the Jewish beliefs of that time. Then his first miracle was to cast out an unclean spirit at Capernaum — an act which was followed by many exorcisms, culminating in the healing of the Gerasene demoniac who had 'legion' or six thousand demons, which provided an astonishing demonstration of Jesus' authority and power over evil. (Mark 5.1–13).

Such a picture of a world inhabited by spirits and demons is foreign to us and it is hard to see how it helps us to understand Christ in the twentieth century. It has to be asked how, if Christ routed the forces of evil, we are still faced with the evils of the nuclear threat, the poverty trap, racial violence, terrorism, pornography and so on.

How far do you think the interpretations of the atonement in sections (a)–(d) above help to explain the phrase 'The Son who redeems mankind'? Try to develop some more up-to-date illustrations of the point that the crucifixion shows God's love for mankind. This could be done by actually trying to paint a picture of what the crucifixion means to you. Compile a list of extracts from hymns to illustrate various views of the atonement. Start by looking at 'Love's redeeming work is done', 'There is a green hill far away', and 'O crucified Redeemer'.

Each of these theories of the atonement has its weaknesses, and none fully answers the question of the meaning of Christ's death, but in a sense its meaning cannot be captured in a definition — it is more to do with our personal response to it. That is to say, the atonement is about being at one with God in such a way that gives positive hope in the face of the negative forces of evil; about accepting suffering as a natural part of human experience, shared by God himself; about knowing yourself, your faults, weaknesses and failures, and being able to feel the forgiving reality of God's presence in your life.

3. The Holy Spirit, who gives life to the people of God

The Holy Spirit is most commonly thought of as the power of God active in the world. The experience of the first Christians at Pentecost was that *power* came upon them, and at the end of Luke's gospel Jesus tells his disciples to stay in Jerusalem 'until you are clothed with power from on high'.

Yet the way in which the Holy Spirit works has always been a puzzle to believers, and they have used a wide variety of pictures in trying to describe his work. Fire, and wind, and a dove descending, immediately spring to mind. So does St Paul's list of the fruits of the Spirit (Galatians 5. 22):

love,
joy and
peace

and his list of the gifts of the Spirit (1 Cor. 12):

utterance of wisdom,
utterance of knowledge,
faith,
healing,
miracles,
prophecy,
speaking and
interpreting tongues.

Sometimes people claim that the Holy Spirit directs them to act in a particular way. For example, a person who wishes to become a minister of the Church might say that the Holy Spirit has directed him or her to make this decision.

In John, chapter 14, Jesus refers to the 'Spirit of truth' and calls him 'counsellor'. This means that

---

The Holy Spirit has the power to show us what is right and true.

the Holy Spirit has the power to show us what is right and true, and also that he acts as a kind of barrister in a law court who argues our case before God. In one sense this is what is meant when the baptismal creed says that he 'gives life to the people of God' because he is arguing before God that each of us should enjoy that quality of life that we call 'eternal'.

However, the most ancient picture for the Holy Spirit is that of breath or wind. In the creation story (Genesis 2. 7) when God made Adam he 'breathed into his nostrils the breath of life'. In that sense God literally gave life to man, and in a metaphorical way he gives life to us spiritually by breathing his Holy Spirit into us.

It is also important to compare this sentence of the baptismal creed with paragraph three of the Nicene Creed (ASB p. 124) where it says:

*We believe in the Holy Spirit,
the Lord, the giver of life,
who proceeds from the Father
and the Son.*

The Christians who wrote that creed believed that the Holy Spirit existed from the beginning of time, just as Christ, the Word of God, did, and that the Father, Son and Holy Spirit together form the creative force behind all life. The idea that the Holy Spirit proceeds from the Father and the Son is that the Spirit has always been a part of God. If we think of the breath proceeding from God's mouth, then we have a picture of what is meant.

CONCLUSION

It is important to remember that the Father, Son and Holy Spirit are not three different gods, but aspects of the one God. They happen to be the particular forms in which men and women have experienced God during the course of history.

Two more ideas for drama

(a) What would the conversation have been about at the Last Supper? Presumably there were several private conversations involving just two or three people. Did they all arrive at once? What were they doing beforehand? What did they understand by Jesus' words 'This is my body' and 'This is my blood'? What of Judas' sudden departure? Read Mark 14.12–26; Matthew 26.17–30; Luke 22.7–23. Make a short play on the 'Last Supper'.

(b) Read Acts 2 which tells the story of Pentecost. Discuss how the Holy Spirit affected the lives of the first Christians and find other evidence in the New Testament for the work of the Spirit. What actually happened at Pentecost? Are there any modern experiences to compare with Pentecost?

2. THE BIBLE

Not many Christians, if we are honest, read their Bibles every day. However, it is important to recognize that the Bible is the book on which the Christian Faith is founded, and therefore a Christian ought to give an adequate amount of time to studying it.

Although passages from the Bible are read at every service of worship in church, it is not enough to rely on these readings to get to know the Bible, because they are usually short extracts, and it is sometimes difficult to understand them outside the context of the book from which they are taken. Apart from that we often find it hard to concentrate on what is being read out loud, and it is much easier to read it for ourselves. Some churches provide Bibles so that the congregation can follow what is being read, which is a help, and the ASB provides all the eucharistic readings for the year on pages 397–978.

Do an experiment by asking yourself at the end of a service what the readings have been about.

What is the Bible?
The word 'Bible' comes from Latin and means quite simply 'The Book'. It is for Christians the Book above all other books because it contains the story of Jesus Christ written by people who actually witnessed the events which led up to the coming of Jesus, and by those who knew Jesus himself. In fact it is more like a library than a single book, containing thirty-nine separate books in the Old Testament and twenty-seven books in the New Testament.

The Old Testament describes the history of Israel over a period of a thousand years from the Exodus from Egypt under the leadership of Moses in about 1250 BC, to references in the Book of Daniel to events in the second century before Christ. Although it is Jewish history it is important for Christians because it gives many examples of God's power to intervene in human affairs, and also contains prophecy which points to the coming of a Saviour, who we believe was Christ himself. Look, for example at Isaiah 9.6, 7; and 11.1–9.

The New Testament is in a sense a fulfilment of the Old Testament. Jesus himself said (Matthew 5.17) 'Think not that I have come to abolish the law and the prophets: I have come not to abolish them but to fulfil them' — and by 'law and prophets', of course, he referred to the Old Testament, because it contains those writings.

The New Testament records the events of Jesus' life and his teachings as remembered by people who actually saw them happen and heard him preach. This information is contained principally in the four gospels — Matthew, Mark, Luke and John.

In addition, the Acts of the Apostles, which was written by Luke and is an extension of his gospel, tells the story of the growth of the Christian Church immediately after the ascension of Jesus. It recounts the great influence that the Holy Spirit had on the first Christians, and the mission of Paul and his various assistants as they converted gentiles to Christianity and spread the Faith around the Mediterranean area.

The New Testament also contains a collection of letters, written mainly by Paul, to Christians in centres other than Jerusalem, like Rome, Corinth and Ephesus. In these letters we discover the kind of moral and spiritual questions which worried the first Christians (cf 1 Corinthians 8), and a deepening understanding of the meaning of Christ and his life. (cf. Romans 5.6–11; and Colossians 1.15–20).

The Bible is the only source of information about the historical Jesus.

The Authority of the Bible
The Bible has unique authority for Christians because it is the only source of information about the historical Jesus. We believe that Jesus was the Son of God, and it is because Jesus has the authority of God that we accept the Bible as authoritative, especially where it records the teachings of Jesus, and the Apostles' interpretations of his importance.

To illustrate the meaning of the word 'authority' in this context, suppose you ask the question: 'What gives authority to any particular Christian teaching?' The answer would be that Christ does and that we discover his will by studying the New Testament.

Is the Bible literally true?
It is a generally accepted Christian teaching that the Bible was inspired by the Holy Spirit of God. But what does that mean? Some have argued that in a mysterious way the Holy Spirit guided the hand of each of the biblical writers so that the words were not theirs but God's — rather like the Ten Commandments given to Moses on tablets of stone. Another, and more easily acceptable view, is that the Bible is inspired because it is a faithful attempt by religious people to record the mighty acts of God that brought about our salvation.

But if it is inspired, is it therefore true? On the 'guided hand' theory it must be literally true in every part because, in effect, God wrote it. However, on the 'faithful-record-of-God's acts' theory it can contain the truth, even if it is not literally true in every detail.

Take the most obvious and famous example — the creation story in Genesis 1–3. Do you believe that God made the world in six days and placed a man and a woman in the Garden of Eden, or do you believe in the theory of man's evolution over millions of years? And if you accept evolution, does this mean that the whole Bible is simply a fairy tale and not to be trusted? No. First because the Bible contains many different types of writing, some intended to be historical and some poetic in character, and secondly because truth can be conveyed by stories. Jesus' parables did not actually happen, but they contain truth. Similarly the Creation myth did not actually happen, but it is an imaginative story told by primitive people to explain the truth of God's creative power, his concern for mankind, and his desire for faithful obedience.

Scholars have insisted that biblical books should be subject to the same critical analysis as any other ancient book.

Changing attitudes to the Bible
Before the late eighteenth century the Bible was generally accepted as divinely inspired in literal detail, but during the nineteenth and twentieth centuries biblical scholars have taken a far more critical approach. They have insisted that biblical books should be subject to the same critical analysis as any other ancient book, and have therefore tried to discover the exact date of writing; who wrote it; where it was written; what readers or community it was written for; what

political events were happening at the time which might have influenced it; and what source or sources of material the writer used.

The following discussion on the relationship between the first three gospels provides a classic illustration of the work of biblical criticism.

What's with the gospels?

If you read the New Testament you will notice something curious about the gospels. Matthew, Mark and Luke are very similar in style and tell the same stories. Whereas John is different — more reflective, more interpretative of events, more theological.

Just to show what is meant about Matthew, Mark and Luke, here is the story of the Healing of Simon's Mother-in-law as told by the three writers, set out in parallel columns.

Simon's Wife's Mother Cured of a Fever

Mark 1	**Matthew 8**	**Luke 4**
29 And immediately he left the synagogue, and entered the house of Simon and Andrew, with James and John. 30 Now Simon's mother-in-law lay sick with a fever, and immediately they told him of her. 31 And he came and took her by the hand and lifted her up, and the fever left her; and she served them.	14 And when Jesus entered Peter's house, he saw his mother-in-law lying sick with a fever; 15 he touched her hand, and the fever left her, and she rose and served him.	38 And he arose and left the synagogue, and entered Simon's house. Now Simon's mother-in-law was ill with a high fever, and they besought him for her. 39 And he stood over her and rebuked the fever, and it left her; and immediately she rose and served them.

Notice the number of places where the words are identical in each account. If you said that they had copied one another, you would not be far from the

Jesus heals Peter's mother-in-law, mosaic in the Kariye Camii, Istanbul, (14th century)

The first three gospels see the events of Jesus' life in a similar way.

---

truth. In fact, because the first three gospels see the events of Jesus' life in such a similar way, they are known to theologians as the 'synoptic gospels' — which means 'seeing together'.

But how did the synoptic gospels really come to be so similar? On the other hand, why are they so different? For example Matthew and Luke both have extensive and different stories about the birth of Jesus, whereas Mark has none.

These questions raise what is known as the 'synoptic problem'.

It is generally accepted that Mark's was the first gospel to be completed, in about AD 65–70. If that is so, then it looks as though Matthew and Luke both used Mark as a source. In simple terms, they copied from it. But they also had other sources. Matthew and Luke both have beatitudes (Blessed are the meek, etc.), but Mark does not.

The source which Matthew and Luke shared may have been written or it may have been oral. It is code-named 'Q', because German scholars called it 'Quelle', which means 'source'. Matthew's personal source is called 'M' and Luke's 'L'.

So a diagram to show the relation of the synoptic gospels looks like this.

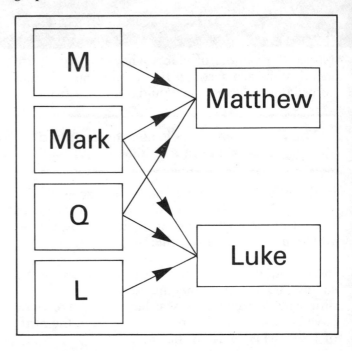

But of course the gospel writers were not so unimaginative as to copy their sources without thinking about what they were doing. Matthew wrote with a Jewish audience in mind, trying to persuade his Jewish readers that Christianity was like a new law or 'Torah' which would very satisfactorily replace the old law.

Luke, who addresses his gospel to Theophilus, which means 'lover of God', and used Greek words, where he could, instead of Hebrew ones, seems to address a wider audience — the gentile world, the world of Greek thought and sophistication.

Furthermore the gospel writers were editors — they didn't just make it up or even necessarily write what they had been eye-witness to. Apart from the

---

Much of the material for the gospels was passed on by word of mouth.

---

sources mentioned, much of the material for the gospels was oral, passed on by word of mouth, and used in acts of worship, in sermons, in debates with Jewish opponents, and in teaching new converts.

What we have as gospels are the final written collections of this kind of material, to give the story of Jesus and the Good News of his Kingdom a permanent form which could be used as a backbone for faith in the rapidly expanding and persecuted Church.

St Mark's gospel
As was suggested at the beginning of this chapter the Bible is a book that we tend to dip into and read short extracts from. However, if you read one of the biblical books straight through you will probably get a quite different impression of what it is about. This is particularly true of the gospels, and Mark's gospel is a good one to start with because it is the shortest, and more importantly it was the first one to be written.

31

The word gospel means God's story.

The word gospel means 'God's story' — that is the story of God's love shown to us through the life, death and resurrection of his Son, Jesus Christ.

The following notes give an idea of what the gospel contains and the order in which events happened. They also try to answer the questions: 'Who was Mark?' and 'Why did he write a gospel?'

If you want more detailed information you will need to read a commentary like *The Gospel of St Mark* by D.E. Nineham (published by Penguin Books). A helpful introduction to the gospels is *The Synoptic Gospels* by H.A. Guy (published by Macmillan).

The lion-symbol of Mark's gospel

A BRIEF INTRODUCTION TO ST MARK'S GOSPEL

The first sentence of Mark's gospel makes it quite clear what the book is all about. 'The beginning of the gospel of Jesus Christ, the Son of God'. In other words this is to be the story of no ordinary human being, but of the Son of God himself. This is going to be something tremendously important.

Mark doesn't tell the Christmas story — that is to be found in Matthew and Luke — but he starts with John the Baptist who announces the coming of Jesus. John then baptizes Jesus in the River Jordan and a voice from heaven is heard saying, 'You are my beloved Son'. (1.11)

Jesus begins his ministry in Galilee, and immediately makes clear his basic message. 'The time is fulfilled, and the Kingdom of God is at hand; repent, and believe the gospel'. (1.15)

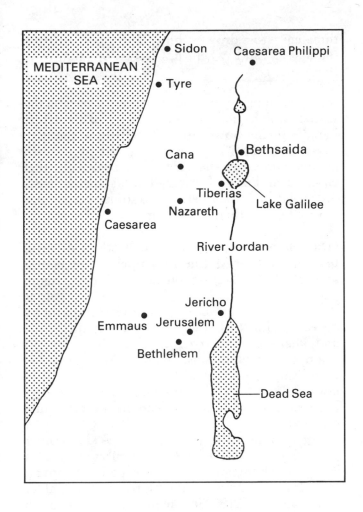

THE MINISTRY IN GALILEE (chapters 1 — 7.23)
Mark describes the work of Jesus. His acts of healing are particularly remarkable, and as a result he gathers a large following. The healings include a madman, a leper, a paralysed man, a man with a withered hand, a deaf person, and Jairus' daughter, who is thought to be dead.

In addition to these 'miracles', he seems to have power over nature when he calms the storm which threatens to drown him and his disciples (4.35–41), and when he walks on the water (6.45–52).

Jesus' teaching is often in the form of parables — stories which make a point. For example the Parable of the Sower (4.1–9) tells how the good news of God's Kingdom is received by different people. Some become very enthusiastic, but their enthusiasm doesn't last very long; some are easily distracted from their belief; and some accept God's call and shape their lives by it.

(One of the most important collections of Jesus' teaching is in St Matthew's gospel (chapters 5–7) and called 'The Sermon on the Mount'.)

It is also important to notice in this section that in his early ministry Jesus began to annoy the Scribes and Pharisees, the strict religious Jews, by, for example, forgiving sins, which they regarded as blasphemy (2.6–7), and by breaking the sabbath laws (2.23–24). This opposition to Jesus was the beginning of what would lead to his arrest and crucifixion.

JESUS TRAVELS NORTH (7.24 — 9.50)
The most significant event of this period happened in Caesarea Philippi, to the North East of Galilee. It is called Peter's 'Statement or Confession of Faith', and it is the turning point or pivot of the gospel story. Jesus asked his disciples who people thought he was, and after several suggestions had been made, Peter said 'You are the Christ'. 'Christ' means the 'anointed one', and the title shows that Peter recognized Jesus as the long expected Messiah.

At the time of Jesus the Jews expected a leader to emerge who would establish God's Kingdom, win back the country from the Romans, and generally make conditions for the Jews more pleasant. This leader would be the Messiah.

After Peter's famous statement, Jesus immediately began to tell his disciples that he would have to suffer and die — scarcely what was expected of the Messiah, who it was hoped would be a sort of guerilla leader of a successful armed rebellion.

JESUS TRAVELS TO JERUSALEM (chapter 10)
Jesus travels from the North down the East side of the Jordan Valley and passes through Jericho where he heals the blind man, Bartimaeus. This is the last miracle in Mark's gospel. However, the incident is of particular interest because Bartimaeus calls Jesus the 'Son of David'. This is the same as calling him Messiah, because the Messiah was expected to be a direct descendant of King David. In other words, Jesus is publicly declared Messiah for the first time.

Jerusalem, The Dome of the Rock, from the Mount of Olives

Jesus entered Jerusalem riding on an ass — an animal that represented peace. The next day he threw the money-changers out of the Temple. Then the Priests and Scribes tried to trick him into speaking against the Romans and the Jewish Religion. For example they asked him whether it was right to pay taxes to Caesar. They did this in an attempt to have him arrested.

On the Thursday he held a meal for his disciples in an upstairs room. At the meal he shared bread and wine, saying that it was his body and blood. This 'Last Supper' is the basis of our Eucharist or Holy Communion.

Later in the Garden of Gethsemane he was betrayed by Judas, arrested, and taken for trial at the High Priest's house. When he was asked if he was the Christ or Messiah, he said that he was. The Jewish officials decided that this was blasphemy and must be punished by death.

Truly this man was the Son of God.

In the morning they took Jesus to Pilate, the Roman Governor. In Pilate's court he was accused of a political crime — of claiming to be a King. Eventually Pilate sentenced him to death and he was crucified. When he died the soldier who was in charge said, 'Truly this man was the Son of God'. This is important because it shows that Jesus' death immediately convinced a gentile of the point Mark wished his gospel to prove, as he said in the first verse of the Book — this is the Good News of Jesus Christ, The Son of God.

Jesus was then buried in a tomb cut out of the rock. Two days later, when several women went to visit the tomb they found the tomb open, Jesus gone, and a young man who told them that Jesus had gone to Galilee and would meet them there.

At this point (16.8) the gospel suddenly ends, almost as if there were a piece missing.

Who wrote the gospel?

That may sound like a silly question. St Mark wrote the gospel. But who was St Mark? He was not one of the disciples, so he did not know about the story of Jesus from first-hand experience. Many people have assumed that he was the Mark mentioned in other parts of the New Testament (e.g. Acts 12.12; 13.5 and 13; 15.37–9). If that is so, his other name was John, he came from Jerusalem and travelled to Cyprus with Paul and Barnabas, his uncle. He fell out with Paul, who refused to have him on his missionary staff and later they were reconciled.

However, Mark was the most common name in the Roman world and there is no absolute certainty that he was the same man.

Mark's connection with Peter

Mark wrote his gospel around AD 67, probably in Rome. In other words he wrote over thirty years after the death of Jesus.

Where did he get his information from? One widely accepted idea is that he was told a great deal by the well-known disciple, Peter. A bishop called Papias said in AD 140 that 'Mark, having become the interpreter of Peter, wrote down accurately all that he remembered of the things said and done by the Lord . . .'.

However we should not imagine Peter and Mark sitting down together, Mark pen in hand taking dictation from Peter. The stories about Jesus' life were very well known and preachers and teachers often memorized them for use in their sermons and lessons. These stories were passed on by word of mouth in worship, in the first century equivalent of confirmation classes, in arguments and discussions. When Mark wrote his gospel he had to edit these stories and put them in order. The story of Jesus' death and resurrection was probably so well known, and so sacred, that he wouldn't have dared alter that at all.

Mark's purpose in writing his gospel

As time passed and Jesus' life, death and resurrection receded into history those people who had known Jesus and remembered his work began to die. It therefore became important to write down as true an account of his life as possible before others began to invent imaginative and misleading stories about Jesus.

Mark's main purpose was to help his own community to believe in Jesus as the Son of God. It is like a sermon, in a way, intended to convert people to a stronger faith.

Read St Mark's gospel for yourself

3. WORSHIP

People will sometimes tell you that you do not have to go to church to be a Christian, but they are wrong. They are muddling Christianity with what might be called 'living a decent life' — which probably means that they try to love their neighbours as themselves, but could mean as little as keeping out of trouble with the Income Tax Inspector and having their children baptized.

However, there is much more to being a Christian than that, and it begins with God. There is a whole area of spiritual experience in which a person has a sense of God's presence, his love, his mystery, and his power, which makes him or her want to respond. It may be a rather nervous, reluctant response, or it may be a positive response resulting in faith, but whichever it is that response itself is the beginning of worship.

Worship means to give God his proper place.

Worship actually means 'to give worth to God'. Put another way it means 'to give God his proper place'. Jesus did exactly this at the beginning of the Lord's Prayer, when he taught his disciples how to pray (Matt. 6.9). He says to God 'hallowed be your name', and with these words he is acknowledging God's special value and holy nature.

If a personal response to God is the beginning of worship, then the worship of Christians together is its climax. Jesus said 'where two or three are gathered together in my name, there am I in the midst of them' (Matt. 18.20), and worship therefore has always been regarded as something that we do together. This is particularly obvious in the Eucharist in which the people of God gather round a table to share in a common symbolic meal. The importance of corporate worship is also underlined by the existence of elaborately beautiful churches and cathedrals designed to house public services.

THE THREE MAIN FUNCTIONS OF WORSHIP

1. To praise God

On occasions — not all the time — we have glimpses of God's power and intuitions of his presence. It might be a sense of his creative love when we see something beautiful in nature; or his forgiveness when we are accepted by others, despite feeling not very lovable; or his challenging love when we are excited and nervous about a new opportunity. In situations like these it is a natural response to praise God. Such moments are the ones which keep faith alive, giving shape to the more ordinary experiences of life.

Unfortunately, the word 'praise' is often used in a sentimental way, as if it ought necessarily to be rather jolly, easy and bright; but to praise someone is to recognize and acknowledge their true value. It may not be easy, and it usually takes a lot of effort. For instance, when a classmate or colleague at work achieves something you have failed to do, like passing an exam or getting promotion, praising them for it can often mean swallowing your resentment and struggling to be generous.

Hymn-singing is a popular way of praising God.

In some ways it is easier to praise God because we are less likely to be jealous of him, but on the other hand we may not feel in the mood, or we may be angry with him for seeming to have ignored our prayers, or simply find that there are more exciting things to do.

There is nothing new in feeling like this — worship has always been a mixture of duty and pleasure. A common modern mistake is to confuse worship with show-business, expecting to be able to sit back and watch it like a television programme, and then being disappointed when it fails to entertain. A better model for worship would be a work of art — a carving, a painting, a poem, a piece of music — because anyone who has tried to create any of these things will know that it is impossible to sit back and let it happen, but that it requires painstaking and sometimes tedious effort. They will also know that pleasure is a kind of by-product of that effort, which often only comes when the piece of art is completed. Interestingly there have been many artists who have thought of their work as an act of praise to God.

God's creative power may be seen in nature

Jesus' parable of the 'Pearl of Great Price' makes the same point when he compares the Kingdom of Heaven with a jeweller who works a lifetime of long hours buying and selling bracelets and neck-laces so that when the immensely valuable pearl comes onto the market he can afford to buy it.

Worship, then, is a duty which we owe to God. Sometimes it will be boring, and from time to time it will be a great pleasure, when all the component parts fall into place and it becomes an inspiring experience through which we discover God him-self.

Look through any hymn book, either new or old, and see how many hymns are hymns of praise.

2. Getting to know God

The second main purpose of worship is to get to know God better. We try to understand his will for us, understand what he is like, and feel his presence amongst us. This is achieved in three obvious ways:

(a) Through prayer.
(b) By listening to Bible readings and sermons.
(c) Through the sacraments.

(a) PRAYER

This is discussed more fully in the chapter about prayer. However, it is helpful to remember that prayer is a two way relationship between God and us. Sometimes it is expressed through words, as in the prayers of intercession, when we try to verbalize our concern for others and ask for God's guidance in social and political affairs, or when we confess the wrong we have done and ask for his forgiveness. At other times we listen to God in silence, trying to concentrate on being in his presence and to feel his closeness to us. It is unlikely that we shall hear him speaking to us in words, but probable that we shall have a sense of his love, or of his approval or disapproval of courses of action we plan to take.

(b) BIBLE READINGS

What the Bible does is describe other people's experience of God.

The Old Testament tells the history of the Jewish religious experience of God and their developing beliefs. The New Testament contains the story of Jesus as told by those who actually knew and remembered him.

Christians believe that the whole Bible reveals truth about God, but that the story of Jesus is particularly important because he was the *Son of*

When you next go to church listen to the lessons and sermon very carefully. At the end of the service try to write down what you have learned about God from one of the Bible readings, and then try to work out the main point of the sermon. Did the sermon explain and develop the ideas expressed in the lesson, or was it on a different topic? Did the sermon teach you more about being a Christian?

42

God. Therefore one of the most obvious ways of getting to know God is to hear the gospel story, and to get an impression of the kind of person Jesus was, and the things he taught. Jesus himself tells us that if we want to understand God better we should look at him. As mentioned earlier he said 'he who has seen me has seen the Father'.

The principal purpose of preaching is to explain and develop the ideas and events that we read about in the Bible. If for example the preacher were to speak about the parable of the 'Good Samaritan', he might explain the geography of the area between Jerusalem and Jericho, the status of priests and levites, the attitude of Jews to Samaritans, and say something about the social conditions in first century Palestine. Then he might establish the main point that Jesus was trying to make through the parable, and apply it to modern life.

In addition to providing biblical explanation, sermons should aim to teach the Christian faith, challenge people to live a Christian life, and provide spiritual inspiration. Obviously a single sermon is unlikely to do all these things at once, and occasionally it will fail to do any of them at all.

(c) THE SACRAMENTS
A sacrament is a sign of God's presence amongst us. It is like a picture or dramatization of his gracious love for us. The two sacraments instituted by Jesus himself are Baptism and the Eucharist.

Baptism
The sign of Baptism is water, and it symbolizes the washing away of sin and the beginning of a new life.

Eucharist
The sign of the Eucharist is bread and wine. When Jesus ate the Last Supper with his disciples, he said

that the bread was his body and wine was his
blood. Many people experience a spiritual closeness to God when they receive the bread and wine
at the Eucharist, and in that way get to know him
better.

There are five other sacraments which are listed
below with their signs.

Confirmation
The Bishop lays his hands on each candidate's
head.

Penance (Formal confession of sins to a priest)
The priest pronounces absolution and makes the
sign of the cross.

Holy Unction
Sick people are anointed with oil.

'The Body of Christ'

The moment of Confirmation

Marriage
The couple make vows, join hands,
and give and receive a ring.

Ordination
The Bishop and other priests lay their
hands on the candidate's head.

3. Being together in a Community

The third main purpose of worship is to be
together as a community. There is an extra
dimension to worship when people are together
which is quite different from private prayer — a
sense of fellowship and mutual interdependence.
The need for this fellowship is demonstrated by the
fact that in countries where Christian worship has
been outlawed Christians still meet together
secretly, even when the penalty for being caught is
execution. It may be of course that a persecuted
church is more conscious of the need for individual
members of the Body of Christ to support each
other, than a church which is widely accepted as
having a place in society. However most Christians
in this country will find themselves in a minority,
especially when it comes to going to church, and
they need to encourage and support each other in
worship, whether they belong to a small prayer
group or a large congregation.

A lax attitude to church attendance is catching —
most of us want to follow the crowd and not to be
the odd one out — and therefore we owe it to each
other to make an effort to attend regularly. It is
very encouraging to see your friends in church, and
the psychological effect is that as soon as one
group is regularly there, others will want to come
too.

But there is a more important reason for worshipping together as a community, and it is that we

discover God in other people. Jesus teaches that we meet him whenever we act lovingly towards the hungry, the poor and the sick.'I say to you as you did it to one of the least of these my breathren, you did it to me.' (Matt. 25.40) The logic of this is that God is to be found in people, including (and perhaps especially) in the weak and unattractive.

All this suggests that worship is a two way process; on the one hand we approach God in a direct personal way, but we also approach him by being loving and open towards each other. In the Eucharist the 'Peace' is the most powerful expression of the communal nature of worship, when people have a chance to greet each other and become aware that they are there not as individuals, but a part of the Church — the people of God.

Different needs in Worship
Finally, we have to understand that people approach God in different ways. There are many

What should your contribution to worship be?

(a) AS AN INDIVIDUAL?
Try to be regular at worship. You should attend your Church's principal Sunday service on average once a fortnight. Occasionally you could read a lesson or help as a sidesman.

(b) AS A GROUP?
Your group may be able to contribute an item to worship. For example: preparing and leading the intercessions, acting a short play to illustrate one of the readings, or a musical item.

If the worship at your church doesn't help you to get to know God better, speak to the clergy and try to develop something which does.

different styles of worship from prayer meetings to cathedral evensong, from high mass to house communion. Each type of service reflects a particular understanding of God and his relationship to his people. A ritualistic and colourful service might emphasize the grandeur of God, his power and mystery, whereas an informal service in which people gather round a simple altar might emphasize his presence amongst his people and the fact that Jesus Christ lived a humble and simple life. Both perceptions of God are important, and neither one is more genuine or spiritual than the other.

Christians need to respect each other's style of worship, and not to think that there is only one authentic way of finding God, which happens to coincide with their particular taste. In fact it is helpful to experience different styles of worship, because each one is likely to help you to understand God in a new light.

Do you prefer to go to a quiet, said Communion or to a Sung Eucharist? Try both and see how each one appeals to you. Talk in your group and try to decide the advantages and disadvantages of both forms of worship.

Conduct a survey of the worship of the churches in your area. Visit three or four different churches and write a description of each service you attend. In your group discuss what appealed to you in each service.

Informal worship at a 'Youth Mass'

4. A GUIDE TO THE EUCHARIST

The Alternative Service Book 1980
In this and the following chapter on Prayer many references are made to The Alternative Service Book 1980 (ASB). This was published in 1980 and as its name suggests is an alternative to the forms of worship in the Book of Common Prayer.

For the previous fifteen years the Church of England had been experimenting with new services which aimed at expresing the Church's worship in up to date language and reflecting the work of modern liturgical scholarship. What the ASB does is to contain these services, in their most modern form, under one cover. In broad outline, the first part of the book contains Morning and Evening Prayer, two versions of the Holy Communion, Baptism, Confirmation, Marriage, Funeral and Ordination services; the second part contains the readings for Holy Communion; and the third part, the Psalms.

Not all Anglican churches use the ASB. Some use the Prayer Book, and some still use one of the experimental Series I, 2 and 3. It is also common to find a combination of uses. For example, the Prayer Book (often referred to as 1662 — the date of its publication) might be used at the early morning Eucharist on Sunday, ASB rite A at the Parish Eucharist, and the Prayer Book for Evensong.

However, the existence of the ASB has not put an end to experimental worship, and many Christian groups find it spiritually helpful to use their imagination in writing their own services for local use.

In your group discuss what you think are the essential ingredients which make up the Eucharist. For example, should every Eucharist contain the Nicene Creed, Bible Readings, prayers of penitence, or an account of the Last Supper? When you have decided on a list of necessary component parts, try to write each section in your own words. The end product could be used at a service in church if your vicar agrees.

What is the Eucharist?

The Eucharist is a commemoration of the last meal which Jesus shared with his disciples on the night before he was crucified. The word comes from Greek and means 'the giving of thanks'. It reminds us that when Jesus took the bread and wine he gave thanks to God before distributing it to the disciples.

It would be useful to read the accounts of the Last Supper in Mark 14.22–26 and 1 Corinthians 11.23–26.

> ' For I received from the Lord what I also delivered to you, that the Lord Jesus on the night when he was betrayed took bread, and when he had given thanks, he broke it, and said, "This is my body which is for you. Do this in remembrance of me." In the same way also the cup, after supper, saying, "This cup is the new covenant in my blood. Do this, as often as you drink it, in remembrance of me." For as often as you eat this bread and drink the cup, you proclaim the Lord's death until he comes. '
>
> (1 Corinthians 11.23–24)

Each of the gospels gives an account of this meal, and so does Paul in 1 Corinthians. However, St John does not describe the actual taking of bread and wine. His account is better known for the washing of the disciples' feet, which is remembered in some churches at the Eucharist on Maundy Thursday evening.

49

In the first three gospels it looks very much as if the Last Supper was a Passover meal. At Passover the Jews celebrated (and still do) their deliverance from slavery in Egypt. It was the custom in each household to kill a lamb and sprinkle the blood on the door-post as a memorial that when, in Egypt, God was to punish the Egyptians by killing all the first-born sons those doors marked with blood were 'passed over'. This is why Jesus is sometimes referred to as the Lamb of God. (cf ASB p. 142 'Lamb of God, you take away the sins of the world'.) The Passover story is recorded in Exodus chapters 11–13.

The modern Eucharist takes its basic shape from the Last Supper itself. Jesus took the bread, gave thanks over it, broke it, and gave it to the disciples. Then after supper he took the cup, gave thanks over it, and gave it to his disciples.

Before these actions take place in our service there are readings from the Bible, with a sermon. A statement of faith, which we call the creed. A confession of sins, and prayers of intercession. In addition hymns and music are often added. It is interesting to note that at the Last Supper a hymn was sung before they left for the Mount of Olives.

Do this in remembrance of me.

In his account Paul tells us that after he had taken the bread and the wine Jesus said 'Do this in remembrance of me', and it is this instruction which has persuaded Christians that the Eucharist is the central act of Chritian worship, because it was instituted by Jesus' own command.

What is the meaning of the Eucharist?
This is a complicated question which has caused much argument over the centuries. Christians have

The Last Supper, painting by Leonardo da Vinci, Santa Maria Delle Grezie, Milan

always believed that Christ is present in a special way at the Eucharist. But how? At the Last Supper, when they took the bread and wine, Jesus said 'This is my body' and 'this is my blood', and therefore people have associated Christ's presence with the consecrated bread and wine.

Christ is truly and spiritually present in the consecrated bread and wine.

There are two prevailing views today. The first is that in a mysterious way that we cannot fully understand Christ is truly and spiritually present in the consecrated bread and wine. This is called the doctrine of the 'real presence'.

The second is that at the Eucharist, bread and wine are simply used as a commemoration, or re-enactment of the Last Supper, in obedience to Christ's command, 'Do this in remembrance of me'. The act of communion symbolizes the close relationship that the Christian wishes to have with God through Jesus Christ, and is a dramatic aid to spiritual understanding.

However there is another aspect of the Eucharist which we ought to remember. Not only is the

How do you think Christ is present in the Eucharist?

consecrated bread called the body of Christ, but St Paul describes the whole community of Christian people as the 'body of Christ'. If we take that picture seriously, then every time Christians are gathered together for the Eucharist — Christ is present through them.

The idea is expressed very clearly in the Prayer of St Teresa of Avila:

> Christ has no body now on earth but yours,
> no hands but yours, no feet but yours.
> Yours are the eyes through which must
> look out
> Christ's compassion for the world.
> Yours are the feet with which he is to go
> about doing good.
> Yours are the hands with which he is to
> bless men now.

So it can be argued that Christ is present at the Eucharist both in the bread and wine, and in the people who meet together to celebrate the Lord's Supper.

The idea of consecration

When the bread and wine are brought to the altar they are just plain bread and wine. (Although many churches use circular wafers of unleavened bread, sometimes with a cross of crucifix stamped on them, which look more like rice-paper than ordinary bread.) However the point is that when they are brought to the altar they are commonplace things. By the time the people receive their communion the bread and wine are treated with special reverence. For example as people leave their seats to go to the altar rail they may bow their heads or genuflect (go down on one knee) as a sign of respect.

So what has happened to the bread and wine? We say that it has been 'consecrated', or made holy. It has become, in whatever sense you understand it, the body and blood of Christ.

When and how does this happen? It is generally accepted that it happens during the Eucharistic Prayer. In the ASB there are four versions of this prayer on pages 130–141. It is a mistake to think that there is any kind of magic in consecration or that the priest has special religious powers which

---

Consecration is God's work, not the priest's.

---

enable him to consecrate. Consecration is God's work, not the priest's. The priest is the Church's representative when he takes bread, gives thanks, calls to mind Christ's saving work (cf ASB p. 132 paragraphs 3 and 4) and subsequently breaks the bread and shares it. The consecration lies in God's response to this act of obedience, because through these actions God comes close to his people.

Some priests put special emphasis on the words 'This *is* my body' and 'This *is* my blood' by speaking them slowly, elevating the bread and wine immediately after saying them, and genuflecting, because they believe that this is the precise moment that the consecration takes place.

It would probably be better to think of the whole Eucharistic Prayer, the whole act of thanksgiving, as the time of consecration.

However it is important to remember that no single interpretation of the Eucharist is absolutely right, but rather that in the experience of a wide diversity of Christian people God comes close to them through their participation in the Eucharist.

Why can only priests preside at the Eucharist?
It may seem odd that the Church of England permits only priests to preside at the Eucharist. Christ gave no instructions that this should be so, and if Christians wish to break bread together in memory of his death and saving work, surely this could be done by any believer. In fact the Baptist

Church and United Reformed Church, for example, do allow any full member of their Churches to officiate in this way, and some Anglicans feel that the Church of England should take the same line, especially in rural parishes where it is sometimes not possible to have a Eucharist every Sunday because there are not enough priests to go round.

Yet from the very early days of Christianity leaders were commissioned by the Church to perform particular tasks, like preaching and teaching. The responsibility for presiding at the Eucharist was given to the local bishop who, it was believed, succeeded the Apostles in leading the Church. As the number of Christian communities grew the bishop was unable to visit them all regularly, and so he passed on this authority to other leaders, called presbyters or priests. This is still the situation in the Church of England today.

Apart from tradition there is another practical reason for limiting the number of people authorized to preside at the Eucharist. By doing so the Church hopes to safeguard its central act of worship from corruption, and tries to maintain the historic pattern of the Eucharist in each community. If anyone were allowed to take the service there would be a danger of the Church splitting into smaller local groups, each with their own eucharistic emphases and peculiarities.

At the Eucharist the priest represents the whole Christian community.

Nevertheless, it has to be said that the priest is not in any way superior to the rest of the congregation, but is their servant. At the Eucharist he represents the whole Christian community, and through training and ordination he is commissioned by the whole Church to do that job. Of course that is only part of his work; he is also trained to preach, lead prayer, visit the sick, advise those in trouble and in most cases to be the full time paid co-ordinator of the activities of the local church.

Step by step through the service

Before the service
Jesus sent two disciples ahead to prepare for the Last Supper. He said that the owner of the house 'will show you a large upper room furnished and ready: there prepare for us' (Mark 14.15). The church building is our equivalent to the upper room, and the clergy and servers get everything ready beforehand — the bread and wine, the vessels, the cloths and the candles. The lighted candles are to remind us of the presence of Jesus, 'The Light of the World'.

It is helpful to be in church some time before the service begins. This time can be spent quietly preparing yourself by prayer or reading, but it is equally appropriate to talk to others in the congregation — these are the people you will be worshipping with. In some churches there is a clatter of conversation until the priest enters.

THE SERVICE
The Order of Holy Communion Rite A, in The Alternative Service Book 1980 begins on page 119 with the exchange of Christian greetings between the president and people.

The prayer at section 3 is sometimes called 'The Collect for Purity'. A collect is a prayer which collects together the thoughts of the worshipper, and here people ask God to help them worship with love and purity of heart.

Prayers of Penitence (sections 5–8)
These prayers may be used either here or later in the service after the intercessions. The particular

value of using them at the beginning is that penitence is an important part of preparation, and they follow on naturally from the Collect for Purity.

Kyrie Eleison (9)
Kyrie Eleison is Greek for 'Lord have mercy', and whether said or sung, the Kyries have an obvious penitential flavour.

In many churches the Kyries are used on Sundays, only in the penitential seasons of Lent and Advent.

Gloria in Excelsis (10)
The Gloria is an ancient hymn of praise to God. It is not usually used in Lent or Advent.

The Collect for the Day (11)
There is a collect for every Sunday of the year, and for certain saints' days. These will be found between pages 397–978 of the ASB.

MINISTRY OF THE WORD (13–17)
The reading of the Bible is the focal point of the first half of the Eucharist, whereas the 'Words of Institution' in the Eucharistic Prayer are the focal point of the second half. For this reason, the framework of the Eucharist is often described as an equal balance of Word and Sacrament.

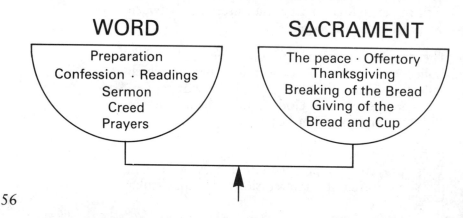

WORD — Preparation, Confession · Readings, Sermon, Creed, Prayers

SACRAMENT — The peace · Offertory, Thanksgiving, Breaking of the Bread, Giving of the Bread and Cup

Poems can be prayers. This poem by Dylan Thomas about the
Eucharist and the crucifixion can be used as a prayer.
Although it is not addressed to God, it is a meditation on
God's sacrificial love.

THIS BREAD I BREAK WAS ONCE THE OAT

This bread I break was once the oat,
This wine upon a foreign tree
Plunged in its fruit;
Man in the day or wind at night
Laid the crops low, broke the grape's joy.

Once in this wind the summer blood
Knocked in the flesh that decked the vine,
Once in this bread
The oat was merry in the wind;
Man broke the sun, pulled the wind down.

This flesh you break, this blood you let
Make desolation in the vein,
Were oat and grape
Born of the sensual root and sap;
My wine you drink, my bread you snap.

There are three readings, one from the Old
Testament, the Epistles, and the Gospels respec-
tively. The congregation stands for the gospel
reading as a mark of respect for the books which
contain the words and deeds of Christ. The same
respect may be emphasized by a gospel procession.

The Sermon (18)
The principal purpose of the sermon is to explain
and elucidate the readings that have preceded it.

The Nicene Creed (19)
A creed is a declaration of belief, and this par-
ticular one is based on a statement made by the
Council of Nicea in AD 325. It has been used

regularly in Christian worship since the fifth century. Its main purpose is to argue for the equality of God the Father, Son and Holy Spirit, and although much of its language is obscure and incomprehensible, Christians value it because of its antiquity.

The Intercession (20)
Intercession means to pray on behalf of others. The prayers are divided into five sections suggesting suitable topics for prayer — Church, World, Local Community, Sick and Suffering, the Departed. It is important for Christians to pray together as well as in their own homes.

Many churches keep a list or prayer board on which 'intentions' for prayer may be written — for instance,the name of a sick person or a personal need. These will then be included in the Sunday intercessions.

The Prayer of Humble Access (29)
The Ministry of the Word has been centred about the lectern and the pulpit, now the focus of the service turns to the altar for the Ministry of the Sacrament. This prayer is a preparation for what follows, and asks for humility in approaching the sacramental elements of bread and wine.

THE MINISTRY OF THE SACRAMENT
The Peace (30)
The Peace provides an opportunity for Christians to greet one another within the context of a service which is otherwise quite formal. Some people shake hands or embrace each other. It is a recognition that they are one community in Christ, and that there is no room for resentment or ill-feeling between those who form the Body of Christ.

The words of Jesus in the Sermon on the Mount provide a fitting text for the Peace: 'If you are offering your gift at the altar, and there remember that your brother has something against you, leave your gift there before the altar and go, first be reconciled to your brother, and then come and offer your gift' (Matthew 5.23–24).

The preparation of the gifts (32)
At the Last Supper Jesus performed four actions — he took bread, gave thanks to God, broke the bread, and gave it to his disciples. This is the first of those actions.

The altar is prepared by the priest, or the deacon, if one is present. Sometimes servers will pass the bread and wine to the priest or, at a main Sunday Eucharist, the elements might be brought from the back of the church by members of the congregation. Such an 'offertory procession' symbolizes the offering to God of ourselves — our work, our leisure, our lives — because the bread and wine are at the same time both gifts of God, and the result of man's work.

The Eucharistic Prayer (38–41)
This thanksgiving is Jesus' second act at the Last Supper, and as the climax of the service is approached there is a sense of the uplifting power of God's presence. 'Lift up your hearts. We lift them to the Lord.'

The prayer begins by thanking God for the redeeming work of Jesus Christ and the life-giving power of the Holy Spirit, and this thanks is summed up in the Sanctus (Holy, holy, holy Lord) which everyone joins in.

The second part of the Prayer is the retelling of the Last Supper story, and contains Jesus' 'Words of Institution'. It is followed by the proclamation 'Christ has died: Christ is risen: Christ will come again', which separates it from the third part of the Prayer.

The third part defines what is being done at the Eucharist — for example, 'we remember his offering of himself made once for all upon the cross' — then calls for the inspiration of the Holy Spirit, and finally ascribes praise to God.

The ASB contains four Eucharistic Prayers each of which follows this pattern. The words of institution are the same in each and the differences are most obvious in the third section.

Every moment of Jesus' life was offered in complete obedience to his Father, and the climax of this sacrificial obedience was his death on the cross. This once-for-all event is brought into the present every time we celebrate the Eucharist.

THE COMMUNION
The Lord's Prayer (42)
'Give us today our daily bread' is a line which takes on extra meaning as people wait to receive the Eucharistic bread.

The Breaking of the Bread (43)
This is the third of Jesus' actions at the Last Supper, and it is sometimes called 'The Fraction'.

Although it is not clear from the ancient sources of the New Testament that Jesus ever described his body as being 'broken for you', it is natural at this point in the service to think of his body broken on the cross.

The Giving of the bread and cup (45–57)

Jesus' fourth action was to share the bread and wine with his disciples. In most Anglican churches the people come to the altar rail to receive their communion from the ministers. The celebrant will probably distribute the bread and an assistant, who may well be a lay person, will distribute the wine. Occasionally, within the context of a more informal service in someone's home or involving only a few people, the bread and wine will be passed from person to person.

AFTER COMMUNION (52–55)

The communion itself is the climax of the Eucharist and after communion the service ends quickly. The emphasis of this section is mission — 'send us out in the power of your Spirit' . . . 'Go in peace to love and serve the Lord'.

In other words the Eucharist is not an inward looking ceremony for the initiated, but a spiritual centre from which Christians can find power to reach out in service to the community. It is a starting point for mission, and not an end in itself.

5. PRAYER

Where do you usually say your prayers? Do you find it easier to pray in a quiet place, when you are on your own? Can you think of times when you could say your prayers?

Prayer worries many Christians because they feel they are not very good at it. We are often led to believe that prayer is a special art which only the most holy can practise. Or we have a picture in our minds of the prayerful person kneeling beside his bed each night for hours on end. But prayers can be said anywhere — on the bus going to school, in the bath, or in a monastery garden. The point is that prayer is intended to help us relate to God, and we should find the method which suits us best.

It is easy to neglect saying your prayers, and unfortunately many people only turn to prayer when they are in special need, for example when a relative is seriously ill, or when things go wrong at school or at work, it is a natural reaction to turn to God for help. When the immediate problem has disappeared, the tendency is to forget God again until another crisis occurs.

Prayer is developing a relationship with God.

God understands our weakness in this respect, and no doubt is glad that we turn to him at all. But as we grow in Christian understanding, we should realize that prayer is not simply asking for things, but developing a relationship with God in which we try to live our lives in co-operation with him.

Different types of Prayer

1. PERSONAL PRAYER

This is the type of prayer which is exclusively between you and God. Often it is called 'private prayer'. It is most likely that you will never say these prayers out loud, but will form them in your mind. This kind of prayer has a natural tendency to concern yourself and those close to you, and you might feel guilty sometimes that your prayers are too self-centred because of the great emphasis in Christian teaching on concern for others. But it is absolutely right to spend time contemplating your own needs and your hopes and fears in the presence of God. All of us need to try to understand the meaning of our existence and it would be a mistake to stem the flow of thoughts about ourselves which we want to share with God.

For example, in personal prayer, we say things to God about ourselves that we would never dream of

---

Prayers can be direct and hard-hitting. We do not have to speak to God in special, holy language. This prayer challenges God with the problem of suffering and evil in the world.

> Father, the news is full of killing and violence,
> And gloomy forecasts about the future.
> It makes me sad and angry to see
> So much misery and pessimism.
> I want to do something about it.
> Surely, your love can change the world.
> I want to be free to
> Enjoy the beauty of creation
> And I want my children to be free after me.
> Father fill me with your Holy Spirit
> So that I may find the confidence and
> Certainty that Jesus is
> The Way, the Truth and the Life,
> And that he will bring good out of evil.

Diana from Colombia receives both the prayers and financial support of a Christian in England

telling anyone else. This is particularly true when we think of what we have done wrong. Pride, deceit, hurtful and cruel fantasies are parts of us that usually we wish to hide from others — indeed we would be ashamed if they were found out — but if we realize that God knows these secret thoughts anyway, it is easier to ask for his forgiveness and understanding.

Although the basis of personal prayer is self-centred, it is very important to pray for the needs of others. Some people keep a list of subjects to be prayed for. It would include individual needs like the names of those who are ill or in trouble, and corporate needs, like world peace, or a Third World country.

As soon as you pray with other people the experience is different.

2. PRAYER IN A SMALL GROUP
As soon as you pray with other people, whether you say your prayers out loud or silently, the experience is different.

The usual pattern for prayer in a small group is that up to about ten people meet in a house or a church room, and after one of the group has said a general introductory prayer, the members sit in silence until someone prays out loud. Usually, the majority of those present contribute a prayer or prayers in the course of the meeting, which would probably last about half-an-hour.

Naturally, anyone new to such a method of praying tends to be shy. You sit there wondering whether you dare join in and worry that you might start and then be lost for words. But beautifully proportioned sentences are not the main object of this kind of prayer, and it doesn't matter if you get your syntax in a twist. God understands, and so do the others present.

Praying together in the Church of Reconciliation, Taizé

Prayer groups were very common in the early Church (Acts 1.14), and the practice of praying in a small group is an important part of the Christian tradition.

> Arrange a prayer group, or prayer time amongst members of your group. But remember, this method is not everyone's cup of tea. No one should be pressed into joining in and those who do should not think they are being holier than those who do not.

3. PUBLIC PRAYER

This is principally the prayer that happens in church and it falls into two categories:
- (a) Set prayers
- (b) Intercessions

65

Read through some of the collects in the ASB and write down one that you particularly like. Then you might use it as part of your personal prayers.

Set Prayers

Examples of set prayers are the collects (ASB pp. 397–974), the 'Collect for purity' (ASB p. 119 section 3), the Eucharistic prayers)ASB 130–141), and the confession (ASB pp. 61 and 120).

These prayers are repeated in the same form day by day and week by week. We come to know them by heart, just as we know the Lord's Prayer by heart, and they become part of our praying tradition.

Some of the prayers in the Book of Common Prayer are of great literary beauty.

Some of the prayers in the Book of Common Prayer, which was used in England for 400 years before the ASB, are of great literary beauty. For example the collect for the 6th Sunday after Trinity:

> ❝O God who hast prepared for them that love thee such good things as pass man's understanding; Pour into our hearts such love toward thee, that we, loving thee above all things, may obtain thy promises, which exceed all that we can desire; through Jesus Christ our Lord.   Amen❞

Indeed the language of the Book of Common Prayer, along with the language of the Authorized Version of the Bible (published in 1611) had a great influence on the development of spoken English. From the Prayer Book we get expressions like: 'the world, the flesh and the devil', 'All sorts and conditions of men', '. . . read, mark, learn and inwardly digest' and 'A tower of strength'.

In public prayer the beauty and accuracy of language is more important because clumsy language can be very distracting when it tries to express the prayers of a large group. For instance, there was a clergyman who when praying for the sick always used to say, 'Father, we pray for all those laid on one side'. Everyone imagined a hospital ward full of patients all facing the same way like tin soldiers. The result was giggling and, although prayer does not have to be humourless, laughing at the prayers is scarcely an aid to worship.

Intercessions
In the Holy Communion (ASB p. 124–125), and at most services, there is a place for a freer style of prayer. At many churches members of the congregation are invited to prepare and lead the prayers of intercession. To intercede means to ask on someone else's behalf. These prayers are therefore primarily for other people.

One of the great advantages of having different people lead the intercessions is that our private prayers are then able to influence our public prayers. In this way a variety of concerns can be brought into public worship. As they are presented members of the congregation will find themselves praying prayers that they would not otherwise have prayed. It may be that an individual will say to himself, 'I wish I had thought of praying that before'.

On the other hand there are pitfalls. No one in the congregation wants to hear a mini-sermon about someone else's pet hobby horse when they are trying to pray. Guidance is needed in preparing intercessions and it is helpful to discuss them with other people.

You and your group could offer to lead the intercessions in your church at the next youth service or church parade. Ask your vicar about this.

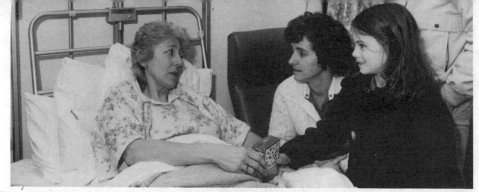

Prayer and action

We have discussed prayer mainly in terms of speaking with God and thinking about human needs in his presence. We could easily be accused of too much talk and too little action. The fact is that prayer should lead to action, and indeed the dividing line between prayer and action is not always clear.

To take the most obvious example. Suppose someone you know is ill and in hospital. Simply to ask God to help that person to get better is not enough. The natural extension would be to visit

---

Your prayer, your visit and medical attention all combine to help someone who is ill.

---

him or her in hospital and to cheer them up in what can be a very boring situation. In addition to this the hospital staff will be giving the appropriate medical care. So your prayer, your visit and that medical attention all combine to help the person in need.

Similarly, you might pray for a farming community in Tanzania which was struggling to produce sufficient food for the population. The natural extension of that prayer would be to try to raise some money to send to Tanzania to help.

Sometimes action is not possible, and prayer alone can easily stand on its own feet, because we believe that if it is his will God can intervene in our lives.

Can you think of an individual that you might 'act' for as well as 'pray' for. Do you know a sick person who would welcome a visit, an elderly person who could do with some help, a lonely person who would like company? Could you and/or your group help to raise some money for a charitable cause either at home or abroad? Discuss it amongst yourselves and share ideas on why and how it could be done.

Confession

This has already been mentioned as the part of personal and public prayer when we tell God what we have done wrong and ask for his forgiveness. But we should look at it in more detail.

Repentance

When Jesus began his ministry he told people to repent (Mark 1.15). By this he meant that they should change their lives and believe in God. There are three sides to repentance. First of all you have to recognize what you have done wrong; secondly, you have to feel sorry for having done it; and thirdly you have to decide to make a serious effort not to do it again. There isn't honestly much point in going through the motions of confession if you don't feel repentant.

The confession in the Holy Communion (ASB p. 127 section 27) mentions not only the sins we have committed as a 'deliberate fault', but also what we have *not* done as a result of 'negligence'. In other words we sometimes do wrong by not taking action. A good example of this is in the parable of the 'Good Samaritan' (Luke 10.30–37) when the Priest and Levite purposely do not help the man who has been robbed and beaten up.

**If we confess our sins to God
he will forgive us.**

Forgiveness

We believe that if we repent and confess our sins, to God, he will forgive us. We can understand God's forgiveness by comparing it with examples of human forgiveness. Most people whether young or old can remember an occasion in childhood when they have, say, broken a plate or an ornament at home, and have been frightened that their parents will be extremely upset and annoyed. If, however, you are forgiven, and instead of anger you receive forgiveness, the feeling of relief is tremendous.

In the Lord's prayer we ask God to 'Forgive us our sins as we forgive those who sin against us.' So forgiving is something which both God and humans do. By sharing in the same activity as God, we should be helped to understand what he is like.

Three styles of Confession
The first two have already been mentioned.

1. Confessing your sins in the absolute privacy of your personal prayers.

2. Confessing your sins alongside everyone else at a public service, using the same words week by week. Sometimes as you say the words particular sins will come to mind.

3. Sacramental Confession. In sacramental confession the person making the confession (the penitent) goes to speak to a priest (the confessor) in private. The confession usually takes place in a church building, and sometimes in a confessional box in which you can hear, but not see each other. The priest will wear a surplice and a purple stole. Before he goes to sacramental confession the penitent will think carefully of what he has done wrong since his last confession, and will probably write down the main points, so that when he speaks to the priest nothing is left out. The priest listens to what the penitent has to say and when he has finished, the sins which have been mentioned will be discussed and the priest will give advice. Finally the priest says the words of absolution or forgiveness.

Remember that your priest is always prepared to discuss any problems that you may have with you. You can trust him — whether you talk informally or in the confessional — and know that he will keep what you say in confidence.

It is important to know that the priest promises absolute confidentiality. In other words he will not tell anyone what has been said. It is also important to understand that it is not the priest who forgives; he simply mediates or passes on God's forgiveness.

This kind of confession, although normally associated with the Roman Catholic Church, is used quite widely in the Church of England.

Is it too formal?
Some people think that sacramental confession as it has just been described is too formal. Nevertheless they see some advantage in talking about their sins to a priest. In this case it is appropriate to talk informally, probably in the vicarage or rectory study.

This traditional prayer by St Francis of Assisi is a beautifully balanced example of how to pray.

O eternal God, in whose will is our peace, we commend
to thee the needs of all the world.
Where there is hatred, give love;
Where there is injury, pardon;
Where there is doubt, faith;
Where there is despair, hope;
Where there is darkness, light;
Where there is sadness, joy;
May we ourselves seek not so much to be
consoled, as to console;
To be understood, as to understand;
To be loved, as to love.
For it is in giving that we receive;
It is in pardoning that we are pardoned;
It is in dying that we are born to life eternal
In thy Blessed Son, Jesus Christ our Lord.
Amen.

---

6. THE CHRISTIAN COMMUNITY

The local Church

Many people think of the church as the local church building because it is for them a physical symbol of godliness, prayer, and religious aspiration in the community. Often the church building is a landmark, standing in a prominent place in the town or village, probably the largest and most impressive public building, and usually of some historical interest, either architecturally or because it contains examples of art and craftsmanship. Often when a church has been threatened with demolition there has been widespread public pressure to preserve it by people who do not themselves go to church.

The church is the people who make up the Christian community.

For worshipping Christians the building is a means to an end — a place in which to worship God. For them the local church is defined not in terms of stones, gargoyles and spires, but as the *people* who make up the local Christian community.

St Bartholomew's, Brighton

This is not to say that worshipping Christians are uninterested in their church building; on the contrary, it can provide a special 'atmosphere' and sense of mystery which is helpful in prayer and although no one believes that God is actually contained within a building, it is sometimes referred to as the 'House of God', and looked after with suitable care.

This care can become obsessive, however, and it is the possessive attachment to buildings and an unwillingness to give them up that is the principal reason why so many small groups of Christians worshipping in the same neighbourhood remain separate, struggling to pay for rising maintenance costs and through lack of co-operation thus weaken the witness of the Church as a whole. St Paul described the Church as 'the body of Christ with many members making up a single body' (1 Corinthians 12.12).

Go into your church when there is not a service taking place and it is quiet. Look around carefully and decide which features you think are particularly beautiful. Are there any parts of the building which are historically or artistically important? Find out about them.

The early Christians did not have special buildings in which to worship. *Discuss the effects that this situation would have upon you and other members of your congregation — how would the lack of a building change your worship?*

Service in the wider community
Although he was the Son of God, Jesus chose to be the servant of those with whom he lived and worked. This was shown in a particularly powerful

Playscheme in action

By listening to the notices given out in church, looking at the notice boards and sheets, and reading the parish magazine, try to assess how involved your church is in its local community.

way when he washed his disciples' feet (John 13.1–11). On another occasion he told his disciples that whoever wished to become great must be a servant of others (Matthew 20.26). Similarly the Christian community should serve others, and see itself not as a self-contained unit for Christians but a part of the whole life of the area in which it exists. The local church should not be a private club for members only, but an open society available to everyone, which endeavours to serve other people — not in an arrogant, do-gooding sort of way, but in a spirit of Christian humility. This kind of openness will be reflected in a variety of ways, and there are some simple questions that can be applied to a particular church to assess whether it is thinking and acting in an open way.

(a) Are local community needs regularly prayed for?

(b) Do any groups exist for 'community service'? For example: visiting homes or hospitals, helping the unemployed, gardening for old people, running a children's holiday play-scheme?

(c) Does the church organize activities specifically for the whole community? For example: an open youth club, a mothers and toddlers group, social events.

(d) Do the clergy visit local schools, factories and offices?

Outreach

A genuine wish to serve the community naturally leads to a desire to persuade others that the Christian way is worth following, because those who have experienced the fulfilment of Christian faith want to share their experience.

The process of trying to bring others to Christian faith is called 'mission' or 'outreach', and it is done in response to Jesus' own command, at the end of St Matthew's gospel where he says 'Go therefore and make disciples of all nations, baptizing them in the name of the Father, and of the Son, and of the Holy Spirit'.

Mission should not be confused with Service. That is to say Service should not be tainted with an ulterior motive like the thought that if I help Mr X then he might come to church. Ideally service

---

The aim of mission is to find the salvation that comes from knowing and believing in God.

---

grows from the love of your neighbour. It is vitally important to realize that the aim of mission is not to get people to join the Christian club, but to help them to find the salvation that comes from knowing and believing in God.

Each local Christian community will tackle the problem of mission in its own way — one will organize a 'mission' with house to house visits, another will hold an annual festival with guest preachers and special events, another will say that the personal example of individual Christians in their daily lives is sufficient. But despite all this it is the openness, commitment to service, and worship of the local church that is important, because mission, like advertising, is wasted energy if the end-product has no attraction.

The world-wide Church
One of the most common and dangerous pitfalls for Christian people is to think of the Church exclusively in terms of the local Christian community to which they belong. Not only does this blinkered, but understandable, view fail to give proper weight to the world-wide nature of the Church, but it also fails to recognize the importance of co-operation and understanding between Christians of different denominations living in the same area.

As a Christian it is important that you should be aware and informed of national and international current events. Try to read a newspaper and listen to news broadcasts as regularly as you can.

Passion Play, St Margaret's Mission, Koriabo

It is of course impossible for a person trying to live a Christian life to be constantly aware of others doing the same in different cultures, different climates and different political situations. Nevertheless, apart from the fact that ideally all Christians are striving for the same goal — namely a love for God which inspires a love for neighbour — they are also linked by a spiritual bond. This spiritual bond, is expressed in the fact that they are all God's people, joined together by prayer, and by the responsibility of being the body of Christ, trying to do God's work in the world.

In the same way as it is important for the Church to be open to society, so it is important for Christians to be open to one another, and willing to learn from one another's experience. For example an English Christian can learn from the person in a communist country who has been tortured for openly preaching Christianity; or from someone who has found Christ in conditions of extreme poverty say in India or Africa; or from an Eastern Orthodox Christian with a very different approach to spirituality from that commonly found in the Church of England.

In practical terms membership of the world-wide Church is expressed principally through supportive prayer. Most local churches pray regularly for the work of Christians in other countries, and it is helpful if this prayer is informed by newspaper reports, and information about specific needs and problems supplied by missionary societies and relief agencies. In addition to this many churches

The address for Christian Aid is 240 Ferndale Road, London, SW9. Write to them asking for details of their publications and newsheets. Perhaps it would be possible for a speaker from Christian Aid to come to talk to your group.

The principal Church of England missionary Societies are:
Church Missionary Society, 157 Waterloo Road, London, SE1.
United Society for the Propagation of the Gospel, 15 Tufton Street, London, SW1.

are able to provide financial support for Christian work in other parts of the world, and for the work of agencies which give aid to developing countries, the poor and those hit by disaster.

Christian Unity
Christian Unity is a blanket term often used to describe the movement within the Church which tries to bring unity amongst Christians who are divided over questions of belief, style of worship, or the organization of the institution. In your own town or village it is likely that there will be churches of different denominations — for instance Roman Catholic, Baptist, United Reformed Church, Methodist, as well as Church of England.

To belong to one particular Christian community necessarily means that a person is part of the inter-denominational, world-wide Christian community. In the past, and to some extent in the present, there has been bitter disagreement between Christians. You only have to look at the history of the Reformation in England (1509–1585) to see this, when for instance people like Cranmer, Ridley and Latimer were burned at the stake during the reign of 'Bloody' Mary for refusing to conform to the teachings of the Roman Catholic Church.

The New Testament emphasizes the unity and equality of those who believe in Jesus Christ.

It is difficult therefore to think of the whole Church with its different member churches and varied religions and social teachings as a single community, yet the New Testament emphasizes the unity and equality of those who believe in Jesus Christ. St Paul sums up this idea in his letter to the Galations: 'For in Christ you are all sons of God through faith. For as many of you as were baptized into Christ have put on Christ. There is neither Jew nor Greek, there is neither slave nor free, there is neither male nor female; for you are all one in Christ Jesus'.

During this present century much has been achieved in ecumenical terms especially between the Roman Catholic Church and the Protestant Churches, so that there is now a far greater understanding of each other's doctrines and a far greater respect for each other's ministry than there was before.

In some local situations ecumenical progress has resulted from congregations of different denominations using the same church building. Usually each congregation has its Eucharist at a different time, presided over by its own priest or minister, but using the same altar, and non-Eucharistic acts of worship are conducted on a united basis. What is more important is that because there is only one building, people from the different churches meet socially, get to know each other, break down the barriers of shyness and suspicion, and consequently their witness to the local community tends to be stronger.

Some young people feel impatient with church government for seeming to stand in the way of church unity.

Youth attitudes to disunity
There are many young people for whom the historical divisions of the Church mean very little, and who feel impatient with church government for seeming to stand in the way of unity. Some will describe themselves simply as 'Christian' and refuse to identify themselves with any particular denomination. For students at college or university this is a comparatively easy position to take because student Christian communities exist in an

environment of freedom and experiment, and because everyone is of the same age there are not the tensions between age groups which often inhibit worship. Consequently it is possible for students to find a degree of unity which would be unusual amongst the churches of an average town centre, including inter-communion between Roman Catholics and Protestants.

However, there are still divisions amongst student Christians of a very basic kind. For example there are those who believe that the Bible is literally true, and those that do not; those who interpret Christian morals in a puritanical way, and those who take a liberal view; those who find God through traditional worship and those who find him through way-out experiment. It is a fact of human nature, and an irony of the whole ecumenical effort of the Church that if a united church were ever achieved, there would still be those who would break away to express their Christianity in their own particular way.

When you visit churches of other denominations in your area note the similarity between their forms of service and the ones you are used to; you will find that many of the prayers are very similar. What are the greatest differences?

Belonging to a Christian community is social as well as spiritual

How do you fit in?

We have looked at the Church as a local, world-wide and ecumenical community, but for those who are recently confirmed the question is how you fit in to your own particular church. This is not always a simple matter, as we can tell from the large number of young people who give up any involvement in the Church within a year of confirmation.

Is it because they were pressed unwillingly into confirmation by parents who thought it was the right thing to do? Or because it was expected of them at school? Or because when a person gets to fourteen or fifteen years old there are so many other attractive activities competing for their time? Or because the church community itself is uncomfortable and unwelcoming, frowning at jeans and coloured hair, and attaching importance to the traditional trapping of religion, like reverent whispering in church, rather than the open celebration of God's love.

It may be that your own church makes it easy for you to fit in by being generally welcoming and specifically by running organizations for young people like a discussion group, a youth club, a community service group, social events, youth services, or a youth magazine. If these are provided, they ought not to be accepted uncritically. Ask yourself whether they really help you to live a Christian life, and whether activities exclusively for people of a certain age create a barrier between different age groups.

On the other hand, it may not be at all obvious where you fit it. You may feel that the activities and general approach of your church community are not relevant to your needs, out of date, or boring. If you do feel like that it does not necessarily follow that you are right and the others are wrong. However you could take the initiative

If you do not see where you can fit into your church community then take the initiative and discuss things with your priest or minister.

80

yourself and suggest what would be interesting and relevant to you both in worship and social activities. Unfortunately some established church communities find it difficult to welcome newcomers, including their own young people, unless those newcomers accept the customs and habits of those already there. Some other churches which fail in this way are full of goodwill, but simply do not know how to adapt to contemporary needs. Keep on trying.

An accepting community
The Church should be an accepting community, and that not only means that it ought to accept you, but also that you must accept others who belong to it. For example it is likely that you will find far more people in it who are older than yourself, which will make a sharp contrast with school. As has already been suggested the so-called 'generation gap' can be a problem, with older people wondering what modern young people are coming to, worrying about their hairstyles, taste in music and perhaps envious of their physical youth and exuberance, and young people thinking the old intolerant, dull and fixed in their ways, perhaps underestimating the experience, abilities, and love of life that most old people have.

It is dangerous to generalize, of course, but between the generations, there is often a clash about what worship and church life should be like. Older people tend to want things to remain as they always have been, while those who are younger want to make changes and experiment. Yet such contrasts of opinion do not only occur between different generations. There are always groups who have contrasting priorities. One will want more opportunity for silent prayer, the choir will want more emphasis on music, a group will fight for social action and money for foreign aid, while the treasurer will probably argue that charity begins at home.

Other people's interests — even their hobby-horses — have something to contribute to the whole.

What is important is that all should be able to accept one another, and recognize that because the Christian body has many members, other people's interests — and even their hobby-horses — have something to contribute to the whole.

Hospitality

There is another way in which the Christian community ought to be accepting, and that is by making everyone welcome. It is easy to be welcoming to those you know and like, but difficult to welcome the stranger, partly because we tend to be shy, and nervous about what kind of response we might get if we speak to someone we do not know, and partly because a newcomer threatens the stability of the group we belong to and feel secure in. This is why cliques develop — exclusive circles of friends which keep others out. However you only have to be on the receiving end of rejection from a group you would like to belong to to realize how unpleasant it is to be excluded, and indeed how cruel people can be in intentionally ignoring you.

The church can only be an open community if Christians themselves are individually open and hospitable.

The Church can only be an open community if Christians themselves are individually open and hospitable. This openness is not simply a matter of plucking up the courage to say hello to someone at the back of the church after a service, but an attitude of mind which genuinely desires other people's happiness; it is Christian love.

Jesus accepted people of many different types and

At the end of a service in church always try to greet people in a friendly manner. Go out of your way to speak to someone that you don't know (or perhaps in the past have not liked very much) and introduce yourself to any newcomers.

82

backgrounds. Amongst his disciples there were poor fishermen, a rich tax-collector, and a political activist, Simon the Zealot. He accepted a leper by touching him, a prostitute by forgiving her, and sinners by eating with them. In short, he broke down social barriers, and accepted the socially unacceptable. This should be a model for the Christian Community.

To its great credit the Church attracts some who find it difficult or impossible to fit into other parts of society — the lonely, the eccentric, the mentally ill. They are attracted to the Church because they expect to find an understanding welcome, and generally they do. They are almost certainly social misfits because it is a struggle to make relationships at all, and the odd mannerisms which result from that struggle are either laughed at or regarded as anti-social behaviour. It is important for everyone in the Christian community to be open to such people, even though it can require great patience, and we may occasionally be laughed at ourselves for it.

Christian stewardship
To conclude this chapter about the Christian community we ought to turn to our own practical commitment to the Church. In many churches today the process of thinking about commitment is known as 'Christian Stewardship', which takes its name from the figure of the steward in the parables of Jesus (Luke 12.42; 16.1) who was a farm manager for an absentee landlord. If we think of God as the landlord and ourselves as his stewards, then we are responsible to God for the way in which we manage our lives. This responsibility becomes real for us when we realize that the air we breathe, the food we eat, and life itself are all gifts from God, and it is natural to want to show gratitude by giving something in return. As we say in the Eucharist '. . . All things come from you, and of your own do we give you.' (ASB p. 129)

But how is our gratitude to be expressed?

1. *Through worship.*

   In this way we are able to show how much we value God's love by praise, prayer, penitence, and the celebration of the sacraments.

2. *Through the responsible use of God's gifts.*

   At a personal level that means respecting other people and their possessions, and being generous with what is yours. At a wider level it raises questions about the conservation of the world's resources, and the distribution of wealth amongst the nations.

3. *Through support of your local church.*

   This is achieved in two obvious ways: by giving money, and by giving your time and ability.

Money
The Church needs money to pay the clergy, maintain its buildings, support the wider Church and those in need, and to run its administration. All these items together are part of the mission of the Church.

Most local churches need many thousands of pounds each year to cover their costs. Put another way, your own church may well need £100 per day. The ancient endowments, or invested gifts from the past, can only pay for a tiny fraction of these costs, and the rest has to be provided by church members, many of whom are extremely generous.

In the Bible (e.g. Leviticus 27.30) tithing was the standard for giving. That meant giving one tenth of your income, and a few Christians still adopt this standard today.

But I'm not earning!
Obviously if you have no income at all it is difficult
to give money. However, most people, even from a
young age, have some money at their disposal, and
it is important to consider how much of this should
be given towards God's work through the Church.
It doesn't matter how small that amount is, so long
as a person has worked it out conscientiously.

In considering your stewardship of money, it is
helpful to set other priorities side by side with God,
like: clothes, sweets, cigarettes, sports club sub-
scriptions, records and tapes, etc.

Time and Ability
These are commodities that everyone has at their
disposal, and the Church relies on extensive
voluntary help and involvement. Can you contribute, for example, by: doing some gardening,
joining a prayer group, writing for the magazine,
visiting the housebound, attending a weekday
service, singing in the choir, serving at the altar,
delivering brochures, designing a poster, doing
some cleaning, planning an act of worship, tidying
the churchyard, helping with Sunday School, or
Cubs or Brownies? All these activities are important to the Church and each member can play
their part.

1. Invite the church treasurer to a discussion to talk about Christian Stewardship
   of money. How much responsibility
   should young people have for the
   finances of their church?

2. List some practical ways in which you
   could help your church, including the
   relevant ones from the list above.
   Choose one of these ideas and set
   yourself a time limit by which you must
   put it into practice.

7. CHRISTIAN ETHICS

Ethics is the study of morality, and morality is about right and wrong. All societies need rules of conduct to help people to live together in reason able harmony. For example in Britain there is a law that you drive on the left hand side of the road, otherwise the road transport system would be chaotic and unworkable. There is also a law that a person should pay taxes, because the Government needs money to provide roads, medical care, and schooling, for instance. If a person gets drunk and drives his car on the wrong side of the road causing an accident, or if he evades paying his taxes we would say that he or she had acted immorally, or unethically.

Christian morality is based on the teaching of Jesus.

Christian morality is based on the teaching of Jesus, and what he taught provides the authority for Christian decisions about right and wrong. For example, he said that is wrong to criticize other people for faults that you are guilty of yourself. (Matthew 7.1–5)

Of course many Christians and non-Christians have very similar or even identical moral standards. That is, they say I am a Christian because I try to live a good and moral life. However the difference between Christian morality and other systems of morality is not so much *what* we do, but *why* we do it.

The motive behind Christian morality
Jesus said 'If you love me you will keep my commandments' (John 14.15), and it is that love of God which is the motive for Christian behaviour. The same point is made by Jesus when he answers the question 'which is the greatest commandment?'

His reply was that to love God with all your strength was the greatest commandment, and the next was to love your neighbour as yourself. In other words, the love of your neighbour flows naturally and inevitably from loving God.

In the past some preachers have tried to frighten their congregations into obeying Christ's teachings by suggesting that to do otherwise would result in eternal punishment. Apart from the fact that it is difficult to imagine how a loving God could condemn people to eternal suffering, such an attitude suggests that we can actually earn salvation by good deeds. However, St Paul denies this view when he argues that righteousness is the result of faith, not of good deeds. (Romans 3.19–26). In other words what you believe is more important to God than what you do, because a personal relationship between God and an individual provides a positive source of fulfilment, whereas an attempt to win God's approval by trying to lead a morally perfect life will certainly end in disappointment and failure.

St Augustine said in a much quoted saying that you can love God and do what you like, which sounds like a very attractive proposition, but is in fact a little more subtle than it appears on the surface. His point is that *if* you love God the things that you actually want to do will be the same things that God wants you to do. So although faith in God is more important than anything else, the true Christian will still try to live his life according to the moral ideas of Jesus Christ.

Christ's moral teaching is limited
Christ's teaching does not give specific guidance on all moral problems, which means that you cannot use the New Testament as a sort of dictionary of ethics. What he said was directed at a Jewish community living under Roman rule in a very different part of the world, nearly two thousand

years ago and naturally some of the moral problems facing those people are remote from our own experience. No soldier for example has the right to force us to carry his belongings for a mile (cf. Matthew 5.41), and if we were on a Sunday afternoon walk in the country we should not expect to get into trouble for rubbing out the grains of wheat from an ear of corn and chewing them (cf. Mark 2.23–28).

But before we dismiss these two incidents as irrelevant to modern life, we should pause to notice that Jesus drew out principles from each which are as true today as they were then.

In the case of the soldier he said that if a soldier were to force you to travel with him one mile you should go two. The principle is that generosity is better than grudging meanness. When we are forced to do a thing we often do it with bitter reluctance like piano practice, or a school subject that we dislike. Similarly some people approach their daily work with a grudging attitude and are determined not to do a stroke more than they have to. Jesus suggests that it is good to give more than is required of you.

The Sabbath was made for man and not man for the Sabbath.

In the second situation, where Jesus and his disciples are criticized by the Pharisees for breaking the Sabbath laws, Jesus draws out a moral principle which is very plain indeed. 'The Sabbath was made for man and not man for the Sabbath.' The point was that plucking ears of corn technically qualified as work, and therefore Jesus was accused of working on the Sabbath. Obviously they were not working but relaxing, and Jesus criticizes the pettiness of the law. The Sabbath was intended by God for man's recreation, yet here the Sabbath law was detroying relaxation. That is absurd. Laws are man's servant, not his master.

This moral principle, that laws must serve not dominate, is relevant to many contemporary situations. For example, a school playground could be subject to so many restrictions that it ceases to be a place where children can actually play, or in church worship it is possible to be so fussy about the rules of ritual that people forget God.

Christ's guiding principles

When moral problems arise for which there is not specific guidance in the teaching of Jesus, it is necessary to examine the problem in the light of the general principles that he has laid down. The most fundamental of these principles is Christian love. Another useful name for Christian love is 'self-giving love', in which a person concentrates on what is good for others and tries to forget what is good for himself. Jesus demonstrated this kind of love in his own life by living very simply, by going out of his way to help the sick and the poor, by being totally non-violent, and finally by accepting the painful death of crucifixion, as it says in 1 Thessalonians 5.10 'Jesus Christ died for us so that whether we wake or sleep we might live with him.'

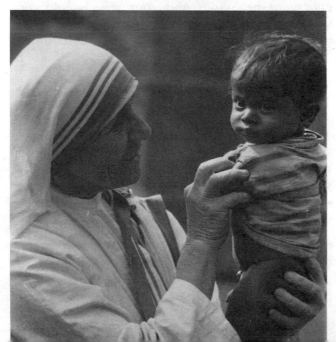

Mother Theresa, who runs Sisters of Charity Mission, Calcutta

Three aspects of Christian love

1. How do you think Christians can show their love for God? Can you think of any twentieth century Christians who have demonstrated their love for God in the way they lived?

2. Loving your neighbour. Read Jesus' parable about neighbourliness, 'The Good Samaritan' (Luke 10.25–37). What is remarkable about the Samaritan's kindness to the injured Jew? Why did the priest and Levite, fellow Jews, not help him? What point is Jesus making about neighbourliness?

3. Loving your enemy. Read Matthew 5.43–48. Do you think Jesus asks too much of those who want to follow him? Who do you think your enemy is? Why should you love your enemy?

89

What moral problems worried Christ most?

We tend to think of immorality in terms of obvious offences against society, like stealing, acts of violence or terrorism, drug pushing, sexual offences and the like. Since all those acts are selfish, unloving and hurtful to other people, they are clearly wrong by Christian standards (and by almost all other standards). In the New Testament Jesus does not often speak out against such obvious immorality, but he frequently speaks against more subtle immorality like pride, hypocrisy, anger, greed, vengefulness. He suggests that the great majority of law-abiding citizens, and particularly the religious leaders need to examine their own motives carefully, because although they live respectable lives, God knows what goes on in their minds — and thoughts can be as evil as deeds.

Take the question of racial prejudice for example. If a white youth goes out 'Paki-bashing' he will be punished, or if an employer shows discrimination and breaks the Race Relations Act he will be taken to court, but it is as bad to harbour prejudices inside yourself, because those prejudices will influence your behaviour and your speech, and consequently influence others for the worse. The attitudes of individuals within society combine to affect what happens in that society.

Three common areas of moral difficulty
1. PERSONAL RELATIONSHIPS
All human beings have personal relationships. Those between parents and children, brothers and sisters for instance, are forced on us. Later we make our own relationships through friendships, school, work and marriage.

Christ asks us to love one another.

Christ asks us to love one another, which means to show care, to be concerned for other people's well-being, and to treat them with respect as people created by God. Sometimes it is difficult to love a person, perhaps because we do not actually like them, or because we disagree with their opinions, or because what they want clashes with what we want. This can easily happen between parents and children. For example you may wish to stay out late at a party, but your parents insist that you come home early. What would be the right course of action?

Sex in personal relationships
This is a very wide-ranging subject about which many books have been written. Here it is only possible to mention some thoughts for discussion.

Jesus' teaching on sex
Jesus has very little to say about sex and most of what he does say concerns marriage and the question of divorce.

In John 8.3–11 we read the story of the 'Woman taken in adultery', in which a woman who had been found in the act of adultery was about to be stoned. When Jesus arrived he was asked whether it was right to stone here. His reply was: 'Let him who has no sin among you cast the first stone', and feeling ashamed the men dropped the rocks they were holding and went away.

Here Jesus puts matters of sexual morality into context: adultery is wrong, but there are other weightier sins to be concerned about. What is of equal importance is the fact that Jesus so readily forgives the woman her sin.

On another occasion, in the Sermon on the Mount (Matthew 5.27–28) Jesus says that 'every one who looks at a woman lustfully has already committed adultery with her in his heart'. The point he is making here is that there is more to morality than rules, and before we criticize the person who has committed adultery, or become pregnant under age or whatever, we should look to our own lustful fantasies, which might be expressed for instance in reading pornography, or looking at suggestive pictures. Such self-indulgent fantasies can be as sinful as the act of adultery itself.

Having said that, however, it must be emphasized that Jesus was not trying to make us feel guilty about our natural feelings. He was not saying, for example, that it is wrong to 'fancy' someone of the opposite sex, because obviously it is very often a person's physical attraction that sparks off a relationship.

The Christian Position

There is no certain, agreed formula on the Christian attitude to sex. In fact Christians often disagree with each other about it. For example the Roman Catholic Church teaches that artificial contraception is wrong, but most other Christians find it morally acceptable, and a sensible method of planning a family and restricting the population explosion. Similarly, some Christians say that sex before marriage is always wrong, while others think it acceptable in some circumstances.

The most important Christian principle in understanding the morality of sex is that people should be treated in a personal way and not as objects. The difference can be illustrated by the following situations.

(a) When someone goes to a prostitute for sex, there is no personal relationship between them. It is a commercial relationship in which the customer pays for a service the prostitute is willing to sell. The prostitute is treated as an object, and probably wants it that way.

(b) When a teenage couple decide not to have sexual intercourse because they recognize that the emotional strains of a sexual relationship which has to be conducted secretly might damage their overall relationship, then they are treating each other as people. They are showing care and respect for each other and putting long term interests before short term thrills.

Obviously in some relationships sexual intercourse can express personal love in a particularly intense way. However it always creates responsibilities:

What do you think these responsibilities are? Think about these for yourself and then discuss them with others in your group.

(a) Children. It is important that children should be cared for and be given as good a home life as possible.
(b) Responsibility to your partner.
(c) Responsibility to others in society.

Marriage
The idea of Christian Marriage is described in the introduction to the marriage service. Here is an extract from the ASB service:

Marriage is a gift of God.

❛ The Scriptures teach us that marriage is a gift of God in creation and a means of his grace, a holy mystery in which man and woman become one flesh. It is God's purpose that, as husband and wife given themselves to each other in love throughout their lives, they shall be united in that love as Christ is united with his Church.

Marriage is given, that husband and wife may comfort and help each other, living faithfully together in need and in plenty, in sorrow and in joy. It is given, that with delight and tenderness they may know each other in love, and, through the joy of their bodily union, may strengthen the union of their hearts and lives. It is given, that they may have children and be blessed in caring for them and bringing them up in accordance with God's will, to his praise and glory. ❜

2. WAR AND PEACE

Jesus seemed to teach a strategy of non-violence in personal and political affairs. He said that we must love our enemies. If someone hits us in the face we should turn the other cheek, and when he himself was tortured and sentenced to death he accepted it without resistance.

Despite this teaching many Christians have fought in wars. Indeed the Crusaders went to war against Islam in the name of Christianity. Furthermore, some Christian hymns use the imagery of war, like the well-known 'Onward Christian Soldiers' or 'Fight the good fight'.

On the other hand some Christians have been 'conscientious objectors' in war time. That means that on grounds of conscience, based on their Christian beliefs, they have refused to join the armed forces, and the laws of our country allow people to take this position.

So there is a moral dilemma: to fight or not to fight. If you fight you have to answer the criticism that the Jewish/Christian tradition has always taught that it is wrong to kill, and that war causes dreadful physical and mental suffering. If you refuse to fight you have to answer questions like: 'Would you stand passively by while your wife was raped and your children murdered?'

Christians have always regarded war as basically evil.

The Just War

Christians have always regarded war as basically evil. However, sometimes it has been necessary to decide whether war might be preferable to an even greater evil. For example, a country might decide to fight rather than live under a ruler who would allow people no individual freedom.

Once it has been decided that war is the lesser of two evils, Christians have traditionally accepted certain guidelines by which it ought to be fought. These guidelines are designed to create what is called a 'just war'.

(a) It must be fought by a properly constituted authority, which usually means a national government.
In objection to this principle you might say that sometimes minority groups are so cruelly oppressed or unjustly treated that they are entitled to fight back through guerrilla warfare, for example.

(b) The cause must be just. This is always a matter of opinion, and you might find it helpful to discuss what circumstances would make a war just. (For example: if sovereign territory is invaded; if a racial group is persecuted; if all the citizens of one country living in another country are executed; etc.)

(c) The aim of the war must be to establish good or subdue evil.

(d) The war must be fought by proper means. This has usually meant that fighting must be between military forces and that civilians should not be involved. Modern weapons make this condition almost impossible to fulfil. In the Second World War the bombing of cities, which obviously killed many civilians, was seen by many as not being 'proper means'.

Smoke mushrooms over Nagasaki after atomic explosion

The Nuclear Question
Modern nuclear weapons have the power to cause mass destruction and to pollute the earth's surface so that healthy life would be impossible for years to come. Because such weapons, if used, could totally destroy God's creation on this planet, many argue that they are in themselves evil and immoral. Additionally, of course, they cost vast sums of money which might be spent on improving the

95

quality of life of the millions of hungry and sick people in the world.

Certainly the theory of a just war makes little or no sense in a nuclear age. The destruction, suffering and social chaos that would result from a nuclear strike could scarcely be seen as 'establishing good', and would surely be more evil than any evil which was to be subdued. Also, the use of any weapon causing mass destruction could not be described as 'proper means'.

Disarmament
Because nuclear war is widely feared and because the stockpiling of nuclear weapons is thought to increase the likelihood of nuclear war, especially by accident, many people favour some form of arms limitation or disarmament. The total abolition, on a world-wide basis, of nuclear weapons is

---

Have you thought about your attitude to nuclear disarmament? Make an effort to read the literature published by both the unilateral and multilateral organizations and consider their arguments carefully. Invite speakers to address your group and discuss their policies with them.

1. CND, 29 Gt James St, London, WC1
2. Pax Christi, Blackfriars Hall, Southampton Road, London, NW5
3. Quaker Peace and Service, Friends House, Euston Road, London, NW1
4. United Nations Publications — available from book-shops
5. The Coalition for Peace through Security, Arrow House, Whitehall London, SW1A 2BX
6. H.M. Stationery Office, Holborn Bookshop, 49 High Holborn, London WC1
7. Study Pack: *Russia and the West — need they be enemies* Shalom, 85 Marylebone High Street, London, W1M 3DE

an unrealistic hope because now that so many countries know how to manufacture them it is very difficult to be sure that such weapons are not being made secretly, despite any agreement that might be made to the contrary. There are two basic theories of disarmament.

(a) *Unilateral*
This is a policy favoured by, for example, the Campaign for Nuclear Disarmament (CND) and it involves one country voluntarily giving up all its nuclear weapons, even though it opens itself to attack by a country which has such weapons.

(b) *Multilateral*
Multilateralists wish to reduce the number of nuclear weapons, but only by all the nuclear powers agreeing to do so equally. Here again there is a problem of 'verification', or how can you be sure that each power is keeping its part of the bargain.

Which policy is the Christian one?
Both policies are justified as proper Christian positions by their Christian supporters. Unilateralism because of the belief in the inherent evil of the weapons, and the hope that a brave one-sided renunciation of such weapons would set a moral example to others. Multilateralism because, given that war is evil, any attempts to prevent it happening must be good. Also we should be equipped to defend the high values of freedom and justice which our country aspires to.

3. DIVIDED LOYALTIES
The third area of experience where we are faced with many moral decisions is that of divided loyalties. To take a simple example, you may belong to a football team that decides to play its matches on a Sunday morning at a time when you

Have you found yourself in a situation where your loyalties were divided. What decision did you make and how did you arrive at it?

normally go to church. What ought you to do in such a situation; leave the team or stop going to church?

A politician may well face a similar dilemma when he finds that his personal beliefs clash with those of the party he belongs to. For instance, suppose the Labour Party's policy is one of unilateral disarmament, but a particular Labour MP believes that a balance of deterrent power is in the long term interests of world peace, does the MP vote against his party and risk his personal standing within the party, or does he compromise his beliefs and toe the party line?

You cannot serve God and Mammon.

Jesus' teaching on God and Mammon
In the Sermon on the Mount Jesus warned against the dangers of divided loyalties when he said, 'No one can serve two masters, for either he will hate the one and love the other, or he will be devoted to the one and despise the other. You cannot serve God and Mammon' (Matthew 6.24).

The word Mammon means 'wealth' or 'property', and what Jesus means is that because God sometimes expects his followers to give up their personal possessions and live a very simple life, a total devotion to wealth is bound to clash with a total devotion to God.

This is made clear in Matthew 19.16–22 where a rich young man asks Jesus what he must do to have eternal life. Jesus tells him to sell his possessions and give to the poor before he becomes a disciple. But the young man could not make such a great sacrifice and he went away sorrowful.

You might wish to argue that to give up all possessions is idealistic and not practical in the social order in which we live. Besides, people need money for food, clothing, housing, transport and so on, and for a person with family commitments, for example, it would be irresponsible to forego material possessions and deny other members of the family the requirements of ordinary living. That would be a fair objection. What matters then is how you use your possession and what emphasis you put on wealth.

In the business world people are sometimes faced with similar decisions. Obviously a commercial company is interested in making a profit, but if that profit is made by immoral means, say by cheating or by under-paying workers, what is a Christian manager in that company to do? If he protests he might lose his job, if he keeps quiet he will know that he is acting against his Christian conscience.

Is it wrong to be rich?
It does not follow that it is necessarily wrong to make money or to be rich. From very early times in its history up to the present day, Christianity has attracted people of all ranks and degrees of wealth from paupers to kings, and it would be difficult to say that any one group has been particularly more sinful than the others.

However St Paul points out that the *love* of money is the root of all evil (1 Timothy 6.10).

There is a deep and selfish driving force in man which makes him want power over others.

Basically, there is a deep and selfish driving force in man which makes him want power over others. Wealth and possessions are not only a symbol of worldly success, but a means of asserting personal power — as they say, 'money talks'. And it is a kind of addiction too; the more you get, the more you want. The great tragedy is that this kind of selfish power-lust can easily blind a person to the needs of the community: educational and medical needs, unemployment, racial discrimination, inner city decay, and of course, on a world-wide scale, the needs (and often exploitation) of Third World countries.

It is not only individuals who are open to this kind of moral corruption, but groups too — governments, clubs, trades unions, churches, states to name but a few. On the one hand an individual can scarcely avoid being morally influenced by the groups he belongs to, and on the other it is very easy to hide personal selfishness by claiming that you have the group's interests at heart. For instance, parents might campaign for better facilities for the school their child attends, knowing that the needs of a neighbouring school are far greater.

Divided loyalties for a Christian in a non-Christian society
Often Christians feel shy and embarrassed about their beliefs and the fact that they go to church. Such feelings may result from being teased about it by school friends or workmates. When people tease or mock it is usually because they do not really understand what Christianity is about. In fact, most people have religious instincts and it is as natural to wonder about God, life after death, and the meaning of existence, as it is to eat and drink. Those who are suspicious of Christianity because they think it is boring or cissy haven't experienced the challenge of Jesus, or understood how many brave men and women have suffered for their faith. And those who are certain that material values are more desirable than spiritual ones probably haven't stopped to consider what in the long run matters most in life. Nevertheless crit-

icism along these lines can be hard to reject and it is easy to go along with the cynicism of the crowd.

Faced with these kinds of pressures Christians can be tempted to hide their beliefs and pretend to be other than they are. However, it is worth asking whether such an attitude is consistent with the teaching of Jesus who said at the end of Matthew's gospel that his followers ought to 'make disciples of all nations, baptizing them in the name of the Father, and of the Son, and of the Holy Spirit'.

1. Discuss the problems of being a Christian in a non-Christian Society. What problems has being a Christian brought to you – in school, at work?
   Think of people who have stood up for their Christian faith against great opposition.
   Find out all you can about Sir Thomas More, Dietrich Bonhoeffer.

2. Hold a debate on the motion:
   This house would sell all that it has and give to the poor. (There should be two speakers for the motion and two against. Each should prepare a speech in advance. A fifth person should be appointed Chairman.
   The Proposer of the motion speaks first, then the Opposer replies. The Seconder of the motion speaks next, followed by the Seconder of the Opposition. A general discussion involving everyone follows, and at the end a vote is taken.)

8. CHURCH GOVERNMENT AND MINISTRY

How the Church of England is governed
To many people the government of the Church of England is a mystery. It is something which goes on in the background, and probably is of little concern to the majority until some controversial issue arises. Maybe the vicar announces that the pews are to be removed from the church, and in the uproar that follows voices are heard asking, 'What right has he got to do that?' Or perhaps a synod decision to give money to a controversial charity will prompt someone to ask, 'Can they spend our money like that?'

The following paragraphs give a short description of the different levels of church government and an explanation of how they are related.

Who decides what should happen in a parish?

---

1. THE PARISH
Who decides what shall happen in a parish? The overall intention is that the vicar, churchwardens and the parochial church council (PCC) should agree together on all policy decisions. However, each have their own particular legal responsibilities. For example, the vicar is responsible for the worship and music in church; the churchwardens must represent the views of parishioners to the vicar; and the PCC has responsibility for the financial affairs of the parish.

The parochial church council is elected each year from those people whose names are on the Electoral Roll of the parish. In order to vote in the election a person must be on the Electoral Roll and attend the Annual General Meeting. The minimum age for joining the Electoral Roll is 16, but it is necessary to be 17 and a communicant to be elected to the PCC.

The PCC must meet four times a year, but in some parishes it will meet as often as once each month. Apart from decisions about finance and the upkeep of church buildings, the PCC, together with the vicar, will dicuss parish policy, worship, charitable giving, issues faced by the Church at a national and international level, and matters of local community interest.

The PCC is representative of the congregation and therefore anyone is free to ask a PCC member to put a question or raise a subject for debate at one of the meetings.

2. THE DEANERY

The Deanery is a group of local parishes under the oversight of an Area or Rural Dean, who is normally a local vicar.

The Deanery Synod

The word 'Synod' is derived from the Greek word for 'a meeting'. The Deanery Synod is made up of all the clergy in the deanery and a number of elected lay people from each parish. They meet about four times a year to discuss matters of doctrine and worship, but primarily are concerned with the mission of the Church in the area.

3. THE DIOCESE

The Diocese is the area administered and governed by a bishop. It is usually about the size of a county and contains many deaneries.

Examples: London (covers London, north of the River Thames)
Exeter (covers Devon)
Newcastle (covers Newcastle and Northumberland)

The Diocesan Synod
This synod is composed of the Bishop and any assistant bishops of the diocese, elected representatives of the clergy, and elected representatives of the laity. It deals with matters of diocesan finance, policy for diocesan mission, and subjects referred to it by the General Synod, or deanery synods.

DIOCESES OF ENGLAND *(based on map published by CIO)*

4. THE GENERAL SYNOD

This is the parliament of the Church of England. It is divided into three 'houses', which vote separately.

(a) The House of Bishops, which includes all diocesan bishops and a few elected suffragan bishops.

(b) The House of Clergy, composed of clergy elcted from each diocese.

(c) The House of Laity, composed of lay representatives elected from each diocese.

The General Synod meets twice a year, usually in Church House, Westminster, but sometimes in York University, and it is responsible for making decisions about the life and work of the Church of England. When questions of great significance for the future of the Church are debated a majority of two-thirds in each house is required. For example this would apply to a decision about the ministry, like whether women should be ordained as priests; or if there were a proposal to change the services of the ASB; or a proposal to amalgamate with another Church.

Ask your priest what are the main issues currently on the General Synod agenda. Discuss them in your group; try to decide how important they are and whether they are relevant to your local church.

The Synod also debates questions on which no practical decision is easily made. A good example of this was the debate in 1983 on the morality and prudence of nuclear deterrence. The debate was called the *Church and the Bomb*.

In 1982 there was a proposal that the Church of England should be united with the Methodist Church, The United Reformed Church and the Moravian Church. This proposal was known as *The Covenant for Unity*. The Covenant was rejected by the General Synod because although the Bishops and Laity voted for it, by a two-thirds majority, the House of Clergy did not.

Synodical Government makes the Church of England a democratic institution.

The relation between General, Diocesan and Deanery Synods
The idea of synodical government is to make the Church of England a democratic institution, and not one dominated by the clergy. It is intended that business should be referred backwards and forwards between the General, diocesan and deanery synods. In this way the thinking of a local church ought to be able to influence decisions made at a national level. In practice this is not easily achieved because of the vast amount of administrative effort needed to make the system effective.

Ministry is exercised by all Christian people.

The ministry of the Church
The most significant point about the ministry of the Church is that it is exercised by all Christian people, and is not the special preserve of the clergy. In other words you are one of God's ministers in just as important a way as your vicar.

The model for Christian ministry is of course Jesus himself, and there are three aspects of his work which provide a basic framework. When he began his ministry he proclaimed the good news of God's Kingdom and called people to repentance; in his acts of healing he showed care and concern for the weak; and in his suffering and crucifixion he showed his willingness to sacrifice himself and his own interests for the sake of others.

These three aspects of proclamation, service, and self-sacrifice are the ingredients of ministry today. Each individual Christian has to work out how to witness to Christ most effectively, whether it be at school, at work, at home, or elsewhere. This everyday ministry is the bread and butter of Christian witness, and more important than all the missions, visiting schemes, conferences and clubs organized by the Church, because non-Christians tend to judge the effectiveness of the gospel by the example of individual Christians as they go about their day to day business. It is always impressive, for example, when someone stands up for their faith against the mockery of colleagues at work. This is proclamation indeed. But proclamation is also the process of teaching and discussion, since the minister must not only inspire people to follow Christ, but also help them to work out what that means in practice.

Service, which has already been discussed in Chapter 6, 'The Christian Community', describes a broad range of Christian attitudes. Jesus said that he was anointed to preach good news to the poor, to proclaim release to the captives, recovery of sight to the blind and liberty for the oppressed (Luke 4.18).

So service includes identifying with the needs of the most underprivileged in society and trying to help both by prayer and action. A modern example of this is the way in which many churches have tried to tackle unemployment by setting up schemes, often with government finance, to provide job opportunities for those out of work. A good historical example is the nineteenth century campaign to abolish slavery, led by Lord Shaftesbury, who was a devout Christian.

Another understanding of service as ministry is to be found in the view taken by many Christians that God calls them to do their particular work in society. Their vocation might be as a plumber, a schoolteacher, a housewife or a priest. In each case it is possible to serve God and man by doing that job to the best of their ability.

The third aspect of ministry, self-sacrifice, was summed up by Jesus as being ready to take up your cross and follow him. Few people are actually called to die for their faith, although it is a

---

There have been more Christian martyrs in this century than in all the previous centuries.

---

remarkable fact that there have already been more Christian martyrs in this century than in all the previous centuries put together. For most of us self-sacrifice is undramatic and involves the discipline of trying to love our neighbours as much as we love ourselves. It is the difficult exercise of giving up selfish interests to put others first.

Lay ministry
Some lay people are licensed by the bishop to undertake special tasks within the Church's ministry, for example, Readers, Lay Workers, and Church Army Officers. To be accepted for such a ministry a person must receive the appropriate training

Deaconess
The Church of England has admitted women to the Deaconess Order since 1861. Deaconesses remain lay people, although they receive the same training

as men at theological college, and in the parish do the same work as a curate, except that they are not allowed to preside at the Eucharist or conduct marriages.

The General Synod is preparing legislation to make a single diaconate for deaconesses and male deacons.

Local Lay Ministry
There are a variety of specialized lay ministries such as lay pastor, counsellor and group leader for which it is possible to train, and in some dioceses these ministries are recognized by the award of a bishop's certificate. But whereas credit should be given where credit is due, the Church has to be careful not to create a hierarchy amongst Christians in which one aspect of ministry is made to appear more important than another. Although it is certainly true that lay people have always served God by undertaking a variety of roles like visiting

---

There is an increasing desire amongst the laity to share in the leadership of the Church

---

the sick, providing music, caring for church buildings, and witnessing to Christ in their lives, there is an increasing desire amongst the laity to share in the leadership of the Church in pastoral work, worship, and synodical government. This is the result of a new awareness of the contribution that every Christian is called to make to God's work.

The ordained ministry

Since the very early days of Christianity people have been chosen and set apart by the Church as ordained ministers. The question of who should be ordained is a decision for both the individual and the church community. In the Church of England when a person believes that he is being called by God to the ordained ministry, he must discuss the

Bishop's mitre bearing the Pentecostal symbol of tongues of fire

matter with his local bishop, and, if it seems right, will be asked to a conference run by the Advisory Council for the Church's Ministry* to examine his vocation more deeply before a decision is taken whether to proceed to ordination.

The majority of ordained ministers are full-time paid parish clergy whose job it is to teach people about Jesus Christ and proclaim his Good News, to celebrate the sacraments, and to lead the community in its worship and mission. All who have been ordained have made a sacramental and personal commitment to God at ordination and the Church looks to them for an example of prayer and holiness.

Different functions in ordained ministry
Historically the structure of the ordained ministry has been divided into three: bishop, priest and deacon. This division is based partly on the pattern of ministry which is recorded in the New Testament, and partly on the different pastoral needs that developed in the growing Church. To understand their relationship it will be helpful to look at each in turn.

Bishop
Originally the title of bishop was given to the leader of a local Christian community. He was responsible for celebrating the Eucharist, and was assisted in his pastoral work by other ministers. However, as the Church expanded the bishop was given the oversight of several local communities, and the celebration of the Eucharist was done on his behalf by priests.

The Apostles themselves had the responsibility of oversight in the early Church, and bishops are seen

---

*For information write to ACCM, Church House, Dean's Yard, Westminster, London SW1P 3NL.

as the successors of the Apostles carrying on their spiritual work through the Christian centuries.

Today the bishop is the chief Christian Minister of a particular area, and apart from his many administrative duties, he is responsible for the spiritual welfare of the clergy in his area.

He is a sort of link man between local communities and the Church at large, and tries to ensure that local Christian teaching is faithful to the New Testament and the traditions of the Church.

Only the bishop may conduct Confirmation and Ordination services. Twenty-seven Church of England bishops are members of the House of Lords, and this privilege gives the National Church a voice in our parliamentary democracy.

Priest
A priest is trained and ordained to be a pastor (one who cares for people like a shepherd cares for his sheep), and a minister of the sacraments; in particular he presides at the Eucharist. An important part of his work is to teach people about the Christian faith and to prepare new Christians for Confirmation.

Deacon
Deacon is a Greek work meaning 'servant'. Its emphasis is on self-sacrificial service in the world, and the care of those in trouble. In worship the deacon is appointed to read the gospel, to expound the readings, and to lead prayers. He may not preside at the Eucharist, pronounce blessings or absolution (the forgiveness of sins).

After training at theological college an Anglican clergyman is made a deacon and begins to serve as a curate in a parish. After a year it is normal for him to be ordained to the priesthood, so that the diaconate acts as a kind of probationary period.

111

There is considerable opinion in the Church of England that the diaconate should be used as a permanent order as it was in the past, that it should include women, and perhaps other ministries like that of lay reader.

The primary function of ministry is to serve others.

Bishops and priests never cease to be deacons. This is to remind them that their primary function, like Christ himself, is to be a servant of others.

OTHER TITLES IN COMMON USE IN THE CHURCH OF ENGLAND

Rector and Vicar. Rectors and vicars do the same job. The difference between them is historical and relates to how their income used to be paid. Each is the principal clergyman in his parish, and is responsible for conducting worship and caring for the parishioners.

Curate. This is the name given to an assistant clergyman in a parish. It means one who has the 'cure of souls'.

Team Rector and Team Vicar. Where several parishes are working together as a team, the senior clergyman is known as the Team Rector and the others as Team Vicars.

Archdeacon. The Archdeacon, who is always a priest, is a diocesan official who assists the bishop in administrative matters. He has particular responsibility for church property.

Deans and Provosts. The senior clergyman of a cathedral is usually called the Dean. Some of the more recent dioceses have used the title 'Provost' for this post.

Canons. This is a title given to clergy on the permanent staff of a cathedral, but it is also given as an honorary title to some parochial clergy, usually in recognition of service within the diocese.

(In some dioceses the ancient title of 'Prebendary' is used in the same way as Canon.)

---

1. *Invite a lay minister (e.g. Deaconess or Reader) to speak to your group about their work.*

2. *Write a description of the ways in which you yourself exercise ministry.*

3. *Is there anyone you know who feels called by God to full-time ministry in the Church? Invite them to discuss their vocation with the group.*

BOOKS FOR FURTHER READING

Chapter 1

The Christian World	Alan Brown	Macdonald 1984
Pilgrim's Progress	John Bunyan	
Investigating Jesus	K.R. Chappel	Edward Arnold 1982
Your Faith	David Edwards	Mowbray 1978
Does God Have a Body	Rosalyn Kendrick	SCM 1977
Can These Dry Bones Live	Frances Young	SCM 1982

Chapter 2

Handbook to the Bible (New Revised Edition)		Lion
How to read the Old Testament	Etienne Charpentier	SCM 1982
How to read the New Testament		
The Synoptic Gospels	H.A. Guy	Macmillan

Chapter 3

Anglican Worship Today — Collins Illustrated Guide to The Alternative Service Book 1980

Chapter 4

I want to tell you how I feel God	Gordon Bailey	Lion 1983
More Prayers for young People	William Barclay	Fount Paperbacks 1977
Home-made Prayers, The ones we did ourselves	Janet Green	Lion 1983

Chapter 5
Masters of Prayer:

John Donne	Mary Holtby	CIO 1984
George Herbert	Mary Hobbs	
Launcelot Andrewes	*Brother Kenneth*	
Julian of Norwich	Pamela Searle	

Chapter 6

The Story of Taizé (Revised Edition)	J.L.G. Balado	Mowbray 1981
Christians with Secular Power	Mark Gibbs	Fortress Press 1981
Who needs the Church	Gerald Priestland	The Saint Andrew Press Edinburgh 1983
Reformation and Society in Six- teenth-Century Europe	A.G. Dickens	Thames & Hudson 1966

Chapter 7

Real Questions	David Field and Peter Toon	Lion 1982
Frontiers	Ralph Gower	Lion 1983
Priestland Right and Wrong	Gerald Priestland	Collins 1983
The Divine Image	Keith Ward	SPCK 1976
The Church and the Bomb		CIO 1982

Chapter 8

Baptism, Eucharist & Ministry	World Council of Churches	Geneva 1982
A Handbook for Churchwardens and Parochial Church Councillors (1983 Revised Edition)		Mowbray 1984

APPENDIX

SOME SUGGESTIONS FOR GROUP LEADERS

Video

This is a resource which is rapidly growing in importance in religious education and is easily available. There is a wide variety of audio visual aid publishers and an up-to-date list of these is provided by the National Society's Religious Education Development Centre, 23 Kensington Square, London, W8 5HN. The Society also runs courses on video resources. The Church's Television Centre, Walton Road, Bushey, Watford, WD2 has a useful hire and free loan service and will provide their Film Library Catalogue.

In addition there is of course a wealth of material which can be taped 'off air' from public broadcasts. However it must be remembered that the copyright laws only allow this to be used for private, domestic viewing. The BBC and ITV Schools' Broadcasts often contain series of short programmes which make good discussion aids. The complete syllabus for school programmes will nearly always be found on the staff room notice board of the local school.

There are two rudimentary rules for using video material: first, always check in advance that it is suitable for your purposes, and secondly, use it selectively. Even when using a complete programme it is often more helpful to stop the tape periodically for discussion, rather than wait until the end when discussion might seem a dull anti-climax.

General Resources

The Diocesan Youth and Adult Education Departments will be able to give advice on resources available locally, and liaison with the RE staff of the local school pays dividends because of their experience and familiarity with modern educational methods. Sometimes the local education authority runs its own RE Resource Centre and it may be possible to make use of this.

The National Society's RE Resource Centre, mentioned above, is also able to advise on books, visual aids and teaching methods. It provides a booklist specifically for confirmation preparation.

Involvement of other church members
Perhaps the greatest resource for confirmation preparation is the Christian community itself. No single person, whether clergyman or layman, need do all the work. It is interesting for instance for the group to talk to church officers about their role in the community and to fellow Christians about their reasons for following Christ or the difficulties of being a Christian in the modern world.

It is important to encourage a questioning attitude amongst young people. At a recent Family Service two eleven-year-olds interviewed their vicar by asking him questions of which he had no prior notice. The questions included: why did the disciples leave their work and follow Jesus? Did Jesus really perform miracles? How do you know that Jesus was real and not a myth? What do you think happened at the resurrection? Why do you believe in Jesus?

* * * *

The following notes provide some ideas for activities which should help to make confirmation preparation more interesting. They are by no means comprehensive and many of them will be familiar. These suggestions are additional to those already boxed in the main text and should be used to complement them.

BELIEF IN GOD (Chapter 1)
Radio Interviews
1. Divide the group into pairs and equip each pair with a portable tape-recorder so that they can interview local people about their beliefs in God. This could be done by talking to the congregation after the main Sunday service, but it is more interesting to go into the shopping centre on a Saturday morning.

   The questions to be asked should be discussed in advance, and the technique rehearsed — it does not have to be very professional. The results can be edited into a revealing tape.

2. Discuss the variety of images and symbols through which people have tried to understand the mystery of God. How helpful are these and what features of modern life might help to symbolize God's power, love, mystery and presence in the world.

Make a collage of images of God using pictures gleaned from colour supplements, verses from hymns, extracts from poems, depictions of fire, wind, shepherds, mountains, a dove, the all-seeing eye, etc., and the group's own creative work.

3. Invite four members of the parish to make up an 'Any Questions' team and ask the group to prepare questions which need not be restricted to one particular subject. This event could be open to a wider audience than the confirmation class.

THE BIBLE (Chapter 2)

1. Show a video cassette about the history and development of the Bible. Include discussion of how the gospel stories might have been passed on and used in the first Christian communities.

2. Ask the group to imagine Jesus as having his ministry in contemporary Britain and to re-write a piece of gospel material in their own words. For example: The Good Samaritan, The Cleansing of the Temple, Peter's Confession of Faith, The Parable of the Great Feast (Luke 14. 15–24).

3. Make a chart of the dates of the principal events in first century Roman history, and Palestine in particular. Then insert the dates of the New Testament writings with a very short description of the nature of their contents.

4. With the aid of a concordance look up references to Simon Peter both during Jesus' ministry and afterwards. What kind of man was he? You could write a pen portrait of his life for a magazine, or act scenes from his life, perhaps using music from *Godspell or Jesus Christ Superstar*.

5. Using photocopies of Matthew chapter 1 verse 18 – chapter 4 ask each person to mark all the Old Testament quotations with a coloured pen. What percentage of the text is from the Old Testament? Read Matthew 5. 17–18. Discuss the nature of prophecy and the relationship between Old and New Testaments.

6. Show Zeffirelli's film *Jesus of Nazareth*. As an experiment read the New Testament accounts of a particular incident in the film. Is the film faithful to the text? Has the film-maker interpreted it correctly?

118

WORSHIP (Chapter 3)

1. Use video cassettes of worship in other religions, and the group's experience of worship to discuss what are the essential characteristics of worship. How important is colour, ritual, being together, prayer, preaching, the reading of sacred books, music, silence, etc? What is the relation between public and private worship?

2. Can anyone in the group play a musical instrument? It may be possible to persuade a few musicians to accompany favourite hymns.
   Unaccompanied singing is very popular amongst young people. Use some of the Taizé refrains, chants and psalms. The result could be presented in church.

3. If there is a hospital ward or old people's home that would like the opportunity to worship, encourage the group to lead a half hour service using their own ideas.

4. Investigate another style of worship from your own. (e.g. Charismatic, Society of Friends, Orthodox, Salvation Army, Roman Catholic). Make a display of pictures and descriptions of its distinctive characteristics. What aspects of it could enrich your own worship?

5. Provide the group with a selection of anthologies of religious verse and prose extracts. Let them choose appropriate non-biblical readings for a special occasion. (e.g. Christmas, Passiontide, Harvest, Christian Aid Week, Week of Prayer for Christian Unity).

THE EUCHARIST (Chapter 4)

1. Meet together for a 'bring and share' meal in someone's home, and plan in advance who will be responsible for which course. Use this as an illustration of the Eucharist. Read the Feeding of the Five Thousand, The Road to Emmaus, the Last Supper Story.

2. Ask the vicar to give an exhibition of eucharistic vestments and explain their significance. Give a guided tour of the sacristy and the church silver.

3. If the sacrament is reserved in your church let the group see the

aumbry, and ask questions about the use of the sacrament. Perhaps in pairs they could accompany the priest on a sick. communion round.

4. Discuss the use of symbolism in our lives (e.g. maps, words, gestures, logos, dress, signs of office). Do some mime in which anger, pleasure, tiredness, illness, sympathy, youth or age are indicated by symbolic gesture. What does the imagery of the Eucharist mean: the bread and wine, the priest's vestments, the offertory procession, the kiss of peace, the altar, the candles, etc?

5. Listen to different styles of eucharistic music from Palestrina to Haydn and Folk to African settings. Note which parts of the Eucharist are traditionally set to music. How does the mood of the music help us to understand the words. Explain why the music is liked or disliked.

PRAYER (Chapter 5)

1. Make a collage of cuttings from newspapers on national and international issues which the group thinks provide an agenda for intercessory prayer.

2. Discuss what people consider important subjects for prayers. Divide into pairs asking each pair to write a prayer on a particular subject and to find a picture that might help to concentrate attention on that subject.

3. Discuss the place of silence in prayer. What is one trying to achieve through silence? Spend five minutes in silence and afterwards talk about the thoughts and reactions that went through people's minds.

4. Arrange for the group to lead the intercessions at a Sunday Eucharist. Let one or two people be responsible for each of the sections (i.e. Church, State, Local Community, Sick, Departed). Emphasize the importance of audibility and timing and discuss the place of presentation in public worship.

5. Visit a monastic house and see the place of prayer in the life of such a community. Alternatively invite a monk or nun to speak to the group.

6. Invite a panel of two or three people who you know to have an

individualistic approach to prayer and hold an interview. Beware of making experts out of them and encourage people to be honest about their failures in prayer.

7. Choose, for example, a Christian Aid project in the Third World. Find out as much as you can about it; find a way to raise some money to support it.

THE CHRISTIAN COMMUNITY (Chapter 6)

1. Arrange for the group to go in pairs to visit members of the parish. They might have a specific research project, like to find out about the history of the local church or gather information about what people expect from the church. The results can be written up for presentation as a display in church.

2. Invite people of a similar age to the group from another denomination to discuss the differences and similarities between life in their respective churches. This could be done formally by everyone preparing a question in advance.

3. Show a film or video of Christian life in another part of the world. Talk about the points it raises.

4. Attend the worship of another church in your area. Make a list of what you liked about it and what you disliked. Try to explain why you felt as you did.

5. Ask a speaker from one of the missionary societies to talk about the work of the society.

CHRISTIAN ETHICS (Chapter 7)

1. Make a video tape of moral issues from news, documentary and current affairs programmes. Material might include for example issues of race, unemployment, industrial action, crime, divorce, drug abuse, etc. After showing each clip discuss the moral issues raised.

2. How should a Christian make up his mind about moral issues. Examine the moral codes of the Bible, particularly the Ten Commandments and the Sermon on the Mount. Make a list of the moral questions that concerned Jesus most, and a list of the principal moral concerns of St Paul in his letters to the early Christian centres. Compile a list of the five most worrying moral problems today.

3. Invite people from different walks of life (e.g. schoolteacher, businessman, or woman police officer) to discuss the kind of moral decisions they face in their work.

4. Identify some of the biblical passages where Jesus points to the Christian's responsibility for the poor and under-privileged. How does this teaching relate to modern Britain? Discuss, for example, the problem of unemployment. What are people's basic rights with regard to work and reward? Can and should the Church influence public affairs?

5. Improvise a series of short scenes in which members of the local council reveal plans simultaneously to close a popular youth club on a council estate because of vandalism and to build a luxury swimming pool in the smartest residential area. What conversations are you likely to overhear in the supermarket, in the street or in the pub? What arguments would be put forward on either side in the council chamber? Invent an interview on the subject between the vicar and reporter from the local paper.

CHURCH GOVERNMENT AND MINISTRY (Chapter 8)

1. Arrange a visit to your cathedral and if possible meet with one of the cathedral clergy to talk about its history and its place in the diocese.

2. Go to part of a PCC meeting. Afterwards make a wall chart of the pattern of leadership in the parish.

3. Take an issue on the General Synod agenda and hold a mock parliament in which members play the parts of, for example, chairman and speakers from the three houses of laity, clergy and bishops. Younger groups may like to dress up and turn it into a play.

4. Make a list of the variety of roles in ministry. Compare it with a description of ministry in the New Testament (e.g. 1 Corinthians 12. 27–31). What aspects of ministry can be undertaken by members of the group?

5. Working in pairs choose an aspect of ministry and make a small project of it. For example: visiting the sick, visiting the housebound, doing a job for an old person, singing in the choir, encouraging a friend to come to church, leading a Bible study.

A competition could be held for imaginative ideas on how to present Christianity in a lively modern way.

6. Invite someone newly out of the theological college to talk about and answer questions on training for ordained and full-time ministry.

INDEX